CHAKRA
MEDITATION

Discover Energy, Creativity, Focus, Love,
Communication, Wisdom, and Spirit

CHAKRA
MEDITATION

Discover Energy, Creativity, Focus, Love,
Communication, Wisdom, and Spirit

SWAMI SARADANANDA

WATKINS PUBLISHING
LONDON

Chakra Meditation
Swami Saradananda

Distributed in the USA and Canada by
Sterling Publishing Co., Inc.
387 Park Avenue South
New York, NY 10016-8810

This edition first published in the UK and USA in 2008 by
Duncan Baird Publishers Ltd
Sixth Floor, Castle House
75–76 Wells Street
London W1T 3QH

First published by Watkins Publishing, an imprint of Duncan Baird Publishers in 2010

Managing Editor: Kelly Thompson
Editor: Susannah Marriott
Editorial Assistant: Kirty Topiwala
Managing Designer: Suzanne Tuhrim
Designer: Gail Jones
Commissioned Photography: Matthew Ward
Illustrator: Helen D'Souza

Library of Congress Cataloging-in-Publication Data Available

ISBN: 978-1-84483-495-2

10 9 8 7 6 5 4 3

Typeset in Perpetua
Color reproduction by Colourscan, Singapore
Printed in Malaysia for Imago

For information about custom editions, special sales, premium and corporate purchases, please
contact Sterling Special Sales Department at 800-805-5489 or specialsales@sterlingpub.com.

Publisher's note: The information in this book is not intended as a substitute for professional
medical advice and treatment. If you are pregnant or are suffering from any medical conditions
or health problems, it is recommended that you consult a medical professional before following
any of the advice or practice suggested in this book. Duncan Baird Publishers, or any other
persons who have been involved in working on this publication, cannot accept responsibility
for any injuries or damage incurred as a result of following the information, exercises, or
therapeutic techniques contained in this book.

This book is dedicated to my dear friend Ganesha
for his kindness and encouragement.

"Within this body dwells the mountain of Meru,
and it is surrounded by seven islands as well as lakes, seas,
hills, plains, and their presiding deities."

Siva Samhita, 2.1

CONTENTS

INTRODUCTION

Chakras are an essential part of the energy body of each of us. How smoothly your own chakras function determines how comfortable you feel in your physical body, how successful your relationships are and how much inner peace you are able to enjoy. By meditating on your chakras regularly, you help to keep them as clean, open and operational as possible, which enhances your physical health as well as your mental and emotional well-being. Chakra meditation is a simple, yet powerful way to develop inner poise and bring your life into balance. In fact, regular daily practice will help you to unlock reserves of energy currently hidden deep within you.

For many years I worked as a teacher and spiritual adviser with a well-known global yoga organization that conducted regular meditation sessions. As part of the curriculum, we suggested that students choose one chakra as a focal point for meditation. If students deemed themselves to be more intellectual by nature, teachers suggested that they select the ajna chakra, the energy centre between the eyebrows commonly referred to as the "third eye". Other students, who felt that they were more emotional by nature, were encouraged to meditate on the anahata, or heart, chakra. Although the lower chakras were mentioned from time to time, they were rarely suggested for the purpose of meditation. After a while, I began to notice how the use of only the higher chakras for meditation tended to leave students feeling too "airy" and "in their heads" at the end of a session. This led me

"Swami Saradananda has striven to maintain awareness of spiritual realities throughout her eventful life, travelling the globe as a present-day renunciate. Thus she is equipped to remind us to keep our focus on our inner worlds using the ancient techniques of chakra meditation."
ROBERT MOSES, EDITOR OF *NAMARUPA* MAGAZINE

to explore meditations on each of the seven major chakras as well as some minor chakras, and to focus particularly on the lower chakras, for their very welcome grounding effects. The outcome was a much more balanced meditation practice. In this book, you will find the results of the many years I have spent meditating on all the major chakras.

Each chapter in the main body of the book focuses on one of the seven major chakras. It begins with an introduction to the defining features of that chakra and is followed by a meditation on its *yantra,* or stylized diagram. By meditating on a full-colour representation of the chakra with its elaborate allegorical images, lotus-flower symbolism and Sanskrit mantra, you can begin to sense the way in which the chakra's energy moves, and learn to feel it within your body. Each chapter then offers a meditation dedicated to the element, or quality, associated with that chakra, from earth to ether. You will also find exercises aimed at eliminating one of the negative emotions linked with an imbalance in that chakra (whether fear, anger, guilt or whatever). These are enhanced by one or two other useful techniques, such as walking and eating meditations or visualization and chanting methods, which are easy to build into your everyday life.

Toward the end of each chapter you will also find a menu of supportive self-help "tools" that you can choose from to enhance your meditation practice. They include flower remedies and crystals to clear your energy channels, essential oils to use in a purifying pre-meditation bath and incense to burn in your meditation space. Dietary recommendations, from grounding foods and herbal teas to fasting, show how to maintain the benefits of meditation throughout the day. Practising yoga postures is a particularly powerful way to underpin meditation on any of the chakras. We therefore provide step-by-step instructions for key poses related to each chakra so that you can build them into your regular yoga practice. Finally, at the end of the chapter, you will find a meditation on one of the associated minor chakras, where appropriate. For example, a minor chakra in the feet is linked with the root chakra and so is covered in chapter 1; a minor chakra in the palms of the hands is connected with the heart chakra and therefore is included in chapter 4.

You can, if you wish, work through the book chapter by chapter, trying each meditation in turn. However, I wouldn't suggest doing more than one exercise in a single sitting. Or, if you prefer, you can practise the themed meditations (such as those on an element) on consecutive days or nights, working across the chapters. You could either begin with the most solid element (earth, in chapter 1) and move toward the more subtle (ether in chapter 5, working up to pure consciousness in chapters 6 and 7), or you could follow the meditations from the top chakra downward, working in reverse from chapter 7 to chapter 1.

Alternatively, you might prefer to simply leaf through the book to find meditations that suit your mood or personality, or that might help you through a particular situation or difficult time. For example, if you have endured a long flight, you might like to focus on grounding yourself using the root-chakra meditation on pages 42–43. If you are scheduled to teach, sing or give a speech, you may find the throat-chakra meditation on pages 114–15 helpful, or if you are seeking an effective way to deal with anger and frustration, you might find the silent meditation on pages 76–77 particularly useful.

The chakra meditations in this book are simple, positive and easy to integrate into your daily life. They offer a down-to-earth way for anyone to discover inner peace, whether you are a complete beginner to meditation or someone already on an established spiritual path.

UNDERSTANDING CHAKRA THEORY

Each chakra constitutes a precious piece of the puzzle of human consciousness. This introductory chapter explains – in terms that are easy to understand – exactly why and how. It does so by outlining the origin of the theory of chakras in ancient India and their connection with the philosophy of yoga – facts which are illuminated by quotations from important spiritual texts. The chapter also helps you to understand the way in which chakras function in your body. You will learn about the principles of the energy body and about the network of channels that distributes prana, or subtle energy, throughout your system. With this knowledge you will be able to appreciate the way in which each chakra forms an energetic intersection between physical matter and your consciousness.

When you can visualize how these whirling vortices of life-force receive, assimilate and express different forms of vital energy, you will feel more able to trust your chakra system – your psychic command-and-control centre – to develop not only your body, mind and intellect, but also your emotions, your spiritual life and your interactions with the world around you. This helps to bring every aspect of your life into equilibrium.

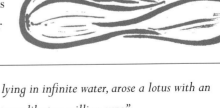

"From the navel of the Supreme Consciousness, lying in infinite water, arose a lotus with an infinite number of petals, lustrous like ten-million suns."
SIVA PURANA, 1.2.34–36

WHAT ARE CHAKRAS?

The literal translation of the Sanskrit word *chakra* is "wheel". Today, the term is usually associated with seven focal points of radiant power, or vital energy, within the subtle body. These are centred around the base of your spine, lower abdomen, solar plexus, heart, throat, forehead and crown of your head, as shown in the illustration below.

Someone with medical training might understand chakras as energetic centres approximating the nerve plexuses in the physical body. A clairvoyant might regard chakras as vortices of energy. A yogi would define chakras as centres of spiritual consciousness. And psychologists use the chakra system to map the development of the human personality. Each is correct.

You may find it useful to picture your chakras as gears that shift energy either down or up. Let's look first at how energy moves downward through the chakras, from the crown of the head to the base of the spine. Think about what happens when you feel inspired: an idea comes into your head; this is crown-chakra energy. As you turn the idea over in your mind, you start to transform it using brow-chakra energy. Convinced that the idea is viable, you might discuss it with friends and colleagues, using throat-chakra energy. Then you "take it to heart" (using heart-chakra energy). You invest energy in transforming the idea into physical reality (solar-plexus

THE SYMBOLISM OF THE LOTUS

Chakras are often depicted as lotus flowers, with each chakra's lotus having a different number of petals. In the Indian tradition, the lotus is a powerful symbol. The plant is rooted in mud and mire, which we can liken to the earth element associated with the muladhara, or root, chakra. The flower grows through water, the element linked with swadhisthana, the second, or sacral, chakra, just as energy ascends through the chakras. The flower's only aspiration is to move toward the sun, represented in the energy body by the crown chakra, the final destination of upward-rising energy. When your vital energy reaches this chakra, pictured as a lotus with an infinite number of petals, enlightenment follows.

chakra energy) and you "water" your dream (sacral-chakra energy) until finally it takes concrete form (root-chakra energy). The more you think and talk about the idea, the more you plan and organize it, the more dense the concept grows with each downward shift through your energy centres until it comes into being. Every building, every item of clothing and every meal began as a thought and followed the same downward movement of energy in order to manifest itself in the world. As you clear your energy flow by practising chakra meditation, the process of making the idea concrete becomes effortless.

However, we also require upward-flowing energy to begin the journey toward spiritual enlightenment. Chakras shift energy in an upward direction, too, making it less dense. As energy travels upward from its base in the lowest chakra (which is associated with the fixed solidity of the earth element), it becomes freer, lighter and less restricted with each step until, eventually, it transcends the elements earth, water, fire, air and ether on its mission to awaken and liberate your consciousness. The exercises in this book help each chakra to function more efficiently, allowing you to get closer to the ultimate aim of meditation: freedom and enlightenment.

HOW DO CHAKRAS WORK?

Chakras function rather like a telephone exchange. Countless wires (*nadi* energy channels; see pages 26–29) feed into the major chakras, each of them carrying vast amounts of energetic information. Fewer "wires" run into the minor chakras. Each chakra takes in and processes this energy before distributing it back out to its sphere of influence, whether in your body or your psyche: chakras are the mechanism by which emotions and ideas affect your physical body and vice versa. In the same way, chakras convey information to and from your senses and your organs of action, which are considered in India to include the hands, feet, tongue, genitals and anus. This means that as you remove energy blockages in your chakras, you enhance your senses while boosting your physical and emotional well-being.

Your lower chakras

Starting from the bottom, your first three major chakras deal with external reality: how secure and stable your life is, how you fit into your community and how you express your individuality:

1 YOUR MULADHARA, OR ROOT, CHAKRA brings grounding and security.

2 YOUR SWADHISTHANA, OR SACRAL, CHAKRA equips you to go with the flow and taste all that life has to offer.

3 YOUR MANIPURA, OR SOLAR PLEXUS, CHAKRA empowers you with the energy you need to function efficiently.

Your middle chakras

Chakras four to six deal with internal reality. They determine your self-perception, and how you express yourself and relate to others:

4 YOUR ANAHATA, OR HEART, CHAKRA governs the energy of love and compassion, enabling you to express love (or blocking its expression).

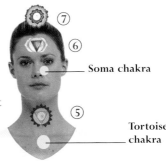

5 YOUR VISHUDDHA, OR THROAT, CHAKRA deals with communication and equips you to take in information and express yourself.
6 YOUR AJNA, OR BROW, CHAKRA is the seat of wisdom. Your mind's eye sees your dreams and directs you to them.

Your highest chakra

7 YOUR SAHASRARA, OR CROWN, CHAKRA deals with ultimate reality and infinite potential.

Your minor chakras

• YOUR PLANTAR CHAKRA, on the sole of each foot, is your primary grounding point and the interface between your energy system and that of the earth.

• YOUR HAND CHAKRA is an essential antenna that enables the world to "touch" you and allows you to keep in touch with the world.

• YOUR TORTOISE CHAKRA, at your upper sternum, allows you to draw mental energy away from the senses and focus within.

• YOUR SOMA OR MOON CHAKRA, above your palate, helps you to taste life's infinite sweetness.

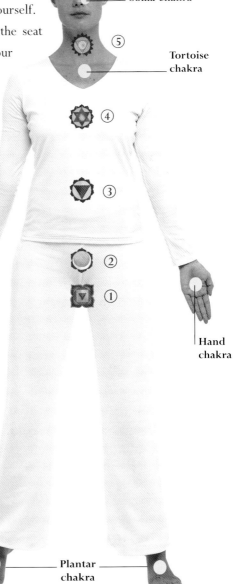

Soma chakra

Tortoise chakra

Hand chakra

Plantar chakra

EXPERIENCING YOUR CHAKRAS

Before beginning chakra meditation it is important to experience your energy centres for yourself rather than thinking of them as philosophical concepts. This will help you to feel where your energy weaknesses and blockages lie, and to understand what all meditation can help you to resolve. In the introductory meditation on the opposite page you take your attention to each energy centre in turn, visualizing each of them as a flower. In the Indian tradition, each chakra is pictured as a lotus flower with a specific number of petals. Start by trying out the sitting position below, which is used in most of the meditations in the book.

Sitting for Meditation

1 *Choose a room that is free from distractions, well ventilated and feels warm enough when you are sitting still. Put on loose clothing, preferably cotton or other natural fibres. Remove your shoes and leave them outside the room. Place a yoga mat or thick rug on the floor.*

2 *Sit on your mat with your legs crossed. Avoid the temptation to sit against a wall or to lie down. Sit tall, keeping your back straight. If sitting this way is difficult, place yoga blocks or a cushion beneath your buttocks, or start by sitting on a straight-backed chair with your feet flat on the floor. Wrap a shawl around you if you feel cold.*

Introductory Chakra Meditation

1 *Sit in a comfortable meditation position with your back straight (see opposite). Take 8–10 full, deep breaths. Then let your breath revert to a natural rhythm. There is no need to try to control it.*

2 *Bring your attention to the base of your spine, the region of your muladhara, or root, chakra. Visualize it as a four-petalled flower.*

3 *Move your attention up to your second chakra, the swadhisthana or sacral chakra, situated in your lower abdomen, around your kidney and genital area. Visualize this chakra as a flower with six petals.*

4 *Now pay attention to the area just above your navel, the location of your manipura, or solar-plexus, chakra. See a flower with ten petals.*

5 *Draw your awareness up to your heart centre, which lies in the middle of your chest. This is your anahata, or fourth, chakra. Visualize this as a flower with twelve petals.*

6 *Bring your attention to your throat, where your fifth chakra, vishuddha, is located. Think about a flower with sixteen petals.*

7 *Draw your attention up to the point between your eyebrows. This is the region of your ajna, or brow, chakra. See a flower with two petals.*

8 *Finally, take your awareness to the crown of your head, the place of the seventh chakra, sahasrara, which has an infinite number of petals.*

9 *Once you feel comfortable with this level of meditation, repeat the exercise but connect the location of each chakra with the qualities that meditation on this chakra develops (see page 18), not with a flower.*

Ending a meditation

At the end of a meditation you may wish to practise the following exercise to ensure that you don't feel too vulnerable. Bring your attention to the base of your spine. Now visualize the flower of the root chakra closing its petals. Repeat with each chakra in the relevant part of your body in turn.

PROPERTIES OF THE CHAKRAS

CHAKRA	LOCATION	NUMBER OF PETALS	ELEMENT	MEDITATION DEVELOPS
MULADHARA *Root chakra*	*Base of the spine*	*4*	*Earth*	• *Root support* • *Grounded attitude* • *Steadiness of mind*
SWADHISTHANA *Sacral chakra*	*Lower abdominal and sacral region, in the kidney and genital areas*	*6*	*Water*	• *Creative impulse* • *Ability to "go with the flow"*
MANIPURA *Solar-plexus chakra*	*Above the navel, in the solar-plexus region*	*10*	*Fire*	• *Ability to adapt and transform*
ANAHATA *Heart chakra*	*Heart region and centre of the chest*	*12*	*Air*	• *Compassion* • *Ability to love*
VISHUDDHA *Throat chakra*	*Throat*	*16*	*Ether (or space)*	• *Creativity* • *Communication skills* • *Ability to overcome limitations of space*
AJNA *Brow chakra*	*Between the eyebrows*	*2*	*Mind (controls the senses and elements)*	• *Intellect* • *Intuition*
SAHASRARA *Crown chakra*	*Crown of the head*	*Infinite*	*Beyond the elements*	• *Spiritual insight* • *Enlightenment*

ANCIENT ORIGINS, MODERN METHODS

The use of chakra meditation as a path to spiritual enlightenment is thousands of years old. It has its roots in spiritual traditions formulated in the Indian subcontinent during the opening centuries of the Common Era (CE). The techniques were passed on orally until medieval times, and written evidence for them dates from the 19th century.

Ancient Chinese traditions share some of the concepts we use in chakra meditation: *prana*, Sanskrit for subtle energy, is referred to in Chinese philosophy as *chi* or *ki*, and what are known as the *nadis*, or energy channels, in the Indian tradition are "meridians" in the Chinese model. However, the Chinese teachings make little reference to the seven major chakras dealt with in this book, perhaps because ancient Chinese interest in energetic principles tended to relate to physical health whereas Indian teachings focused on spiritual enlightenment.

In the modern Western world we most commonly encounter the theory of chakras in yoga classes. Hatha yoga developed in India thousands of years ago as a method of attaining enlightenment. It advocates following eight disciplines in order to gain control over our physical body, our mind and our subtle energy. The first discipline is internal and external purification, the second physical exercise, the third energy-sealing hand and body gestures, the fourth breath-control, the fifth sense-withdrawal, the sixth concentration, the seventh chakra meditation, and the final is the experience of absolute oneness. Increased flexibility, a stronger body and a lessening of the stress that is inherent in modern lifestyles are all positive side effects of this spiritual practice, hatha yoga. Because chakra meditation has been part of hatha yoga since ancient times, breath-control exercises and yoga postures are particularly effective in rebalancing and stimulating chakras, and so you will find that they form many of the exercises in this book.

THE THREE BODIES

To understand how the meditations in this book work and how they can help you in your daily life, it's useful to gain a little understanding of the yogic system of subtle anatomy from which the theory of chakras originates. Yogic theory postulates a model of three bodies: the physical, the astral and what is known as the "seed" or causal body. Each of these bodies is more subtle and less easy to perceive than the previous one. Meanwhile, your true self – which is pure consciousness – lies beyond all these bodies. Trying to understand and identify with your true self is the goal of all meditation and yoga practice. To attain liberation you must stop identifying with the different sheaths, or layers, of the bodies and start identifying with the "self" that is beyond the sheaths.

The physical body

The most concrete of your three bodies is the body you are most familiar with, the physical body – *stula sharira* in Sanskrit – that you refer to as "my body". It has only one layer, the "food sheath", or *annamaya kosha*. (Yogic theory states that it is made up of the food you eat.) This is the body that you were born into and that you have watched grow and change. As you get older this physical body begins to break down, and eventually it will die. After death, its components return to the cycle of nature as its physical structure decays. Your physical body is said to be made up of "gross matter", forged from five elements: earth, water, fire, air and ether (or space). Understanding how these elements relate to the chakras is important in chakra meditation (see chart, right).

"Just as a person casts off worn out clothes and puts on new ones, so also the embodied Self casts off worn-out bodies and enters others which are new."
BHAGAVAD GITA, 2.22

ELEMENTS MAKING UP THE PHYSICAL BODY

ELEMENT	ASSOCIATED WITH
EARTH, or solid matter	ROOT, the lowest or first, chakra
WATER, or liquid matter	SACRAL, or second, chakra
FIRE, or physical energy	SOLAR-PLEXUS, or third, chakra
AIR, or gaseous matter	HEART, or fourth, chakra
ETHER, or space	THROAT, or fifth, chakra

The sixth and seventh chakras are beyond physical elements so have no element meditations.

In this book you will find meditations that purify all five elements that make up your physical body. Following these exercises not only enhances your physical well-being, but also gives you control over your physical body, eventually leading to control of your prana (vital energy). When you can guide your prana into positive channels you can begin to master your mind. To purify and strengthen your physical body further, follow all the breathing meditations set out in the chapters, augmenting them with the *asanas* (physical yoga exercises) recommended near the end of each one. Eating a light, vegetarian diet and fasting occasionally will also boost the effects of meditation on your physical body.

The astral body

Most people who are interested in chakra meditation instinctively recognize that greater dimensions lie beyond the "reality" of the physical body. The astral, or subtle, body (in Sanskrit, *sukshma sharira*) is the second body defined by yogic theory. This is the body that Hindus and Buddhists believe reincarnates, taking a new physical body at birth. Your astral body is believed to be connected to your physical body by a subtle thread while you are alive. During sleep, your physical body lies in a dormant state, liberating your astral body from the restraints of physical "reality". Hence, in dreams you are not bound by time, space or causation; you do not have to obey the laws of gravity or cohesion. You may float through the air, be in London and New York simultaneously, or know something before it happens. But even while you are dreaming or "astral travelling", your physical and astral bodies are connected. Only at the time of death does the thread break, and the astral and seed bodies (see page 24) separate completely from your physical body.

Your astral body is the home of your personality and your thoughts, your likes and dislikes – indeed, this body contains all the qualities and attributes you have that are non-physical in nature. To understand this concept better, think about what happens when you experience love or fear. Although these emotions seem to affect your physical body strongly – for example, by touching your heart or loosening your bowels – they do not actually emanate from your physical body. Where do they begin? In your astral body, where they sit alongside your mind, intellect and prana, or vital energy. So by "retuning" your astral body with chakra meditation you are able to positively affect your personality, thoughts and intellect.

The layers of the astral body

Your astral body is the most complex of the three bodies. It is thought to have three *koshas* – "sheaths" or layers.

• **THE FIRST SHEATH**, or *pranamaya kosha*, is the important "vital" layer that you focus on when performing chakra meditation. The pranamaya kosha contains your prana, the network of channels that this life-force runs through, and the chakras that receive and transmit the energy. This body of prana is the energetic "double" that lies closest to your physical body, its energy flowing through your body and interpenetrating it in

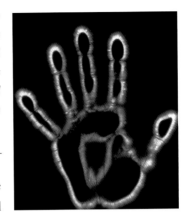

A Kirlian photograph is said to be a visual image of the astral body's first sheath. Chakra meditation purifies and strengthens not only this first "layer" of the astral body, which is pictured clearly on the image and relates to physical sensation, but also the second (mental and emotional) layer, and the third, which is concerned with intellect and individuality.

the same way that water fills a sponge. The five yogic organs of action are also situated here (the hands, feet, tongue, genitals and anus), governing how you react to the world. This is the layer of the astral body in which you experience sensations, including heat, cold, hunger and thirst. You can purify and strengthen this sheath by performing the yoga postures (asanas) suggested at the end of each chapter, by practising conscious silence (see pages 112–13) and by working carefully through all the chakra meditations and breathing techniques set out in this book.

• **THE SECOND SHEATH**, or *manomaya kosha*, is the astral body's mental and emotional layer. This is where you experience feelings such as anger, lust, grief, excitement, depression and delusion. The five organs of knowledge are here (the senses), governing how you know the world and how the world affects you. Also here is your automatic mind, with its conscious, subconscious and instinctive portions. This sheath may be likened to a bank teller or clerk, who carries out day-to-day work in a conscious way, but does not make more intellectual decisions about bank or corporate policy. This layer governs learnt habitual actions, such as stopping at a red traffic light or brushing your teeth after breakfast – habits that have developed over years and been carried out with full mental awareness, but which were initially established by your intellect, in the next sheath. You can purify and strengthen your automatic mind and senses by following all the meditations and pranayama breathing techniques in the book, and by fasting occasionally, chanting, being mindful, performing selfless acts and practising spiritual devotion.

• **THE THIRD SHEATH**, or *vijnanamaya kosha*, is the intellectual layer of your astral body. Think of it as the bank manager or CEO whose job is to come up with and implement the policies you follow in life. It is in this layer that you have doubts, debate with yourself, make choices and pass judgments. As well as being home to your intellect, this layer is where your ego resides. In yogic philosophy, the concept of "ego" is quite different from that of Western psychology. Here, your ego is regarded as your sense of unique individuality: quite simply, it is who you perceive yourself to be. It is also what separates you from identifying with universal consciousness. If you are interested in progressing along a spiritual path, it is important to try to purify your ego while you hone your intellect. You can do this by thinking positively, doing selfless deeds and involving yourself in focused inquiry and ongoing study while you follow the meditations in this book.

The seed body

The third body is called in Sanskrit the *karana sharira*, the "seed", or "causal", body. Yogic theory states that your karma (the consequences of past actions) and all the subtle impressions from this and past lives are stored in this body. It is a storehouse thought by yogis to cause you to take a particular body and family at birth. It determines your talents and aptitudes, your emotional make-up and your physical appearance. This seed body has only one layer, the bliss sheath, or *anandamaya kosha*, where you experience joy and happiness. The most effective way to purify this body is by regular meditation.

GETTING TO KNOW YOUR THREE BODIES

BODY	FORMED FROM	MADE UP OF	EXPERIENCES	PERCEIVED IN	HOW TO PURIFY
PHYSICAL BODY Stula sharira	**FOOD SHEATH** Annamaya kosha	• *Elements: earth, water, fire, air, ether (space)*	*Birth, growth, change, decay, death*	*Waking state*	*Yoga poses, breathing and detox techniques, vegetarian diet and fasting*
ASTRAL BODY Sukshma sharira	**VITAL SHEATH** Pranamaya kosha	• *Prana* • *Organs of action (hands, feet, tongue, genitals, anus)*	*Hunger, thirst, heat, cold*	*Waking and dream states*	*Yoga poses and breathing techniques, conscious silence*
	MENTAL SHEATH Manomaya kosha	• *Organs of knowledge (the senses)* • *Conscious and subconscious mind*	*Emotions, such as anger, lust, exhilaration, depression*	*Waking and dream states*	*Breathing exercises, fasting, selfless service, chanting, spiritual devotion, meditation*
	INTELLECTUAL SHEATH Vijnanamaya kosha	• *Ego and intellect*	*Thought, judgment and decision-making*	*Waking and dream states*	*Selfless service, meditation, positive thinking, scripture-study, self-enquiry*
SEED BODY Karana sharira	**BLISS SHEATH** Anandamaya kosha	• *Karma* • *Deep unconscious impressions*	*Happiness, joy*	*Waking, dream and deep-sleep states*	*Meditation*

PRANA AND NADIS

The Sanskrit word *prana,* which refers to the subtle energy flowing through us, is translated as "life-force", "vital energy" or "vital air". But none of these English terms describes it perfectly because until recently, we in the West did not recognize it as a cultural concept. The Chinese word *chi* (as in tai *chi*) and the Japanese word *ki* (in a*kido* and Reiki) translate the idea of prana exactly, and people practising acupuncture, reflexology, shiatsu and martial arts work with this force.

Prana flows through the physical body in subtle channels known as nadis (in Sanskrit, *nadi* means a riverbed containing water, or the channel through which a river flows; in the Chinese system, nadis are called "meridians".) Approximately 72,000 nadis make up the subtle wiring of your pranic sheath, the first layer of your astral body (see pages 22–3). Just some of these nadis are shown opposite on a traditional Indian depiction of the physical body surrounded by and intermingling with the astral body, and the key major and minor chakras.

You might like to visualize your nadis as roads within an energy highway system. Where two or more roads cross, energy junctions, or chakras, form. The seven major crossing points are therefore the sites of the seven major chakras, while less busy "intersections" form the minor chakras. When your energy highway is free from traffic jams, vehicles (prana) can travel freely, but the more roads that come together, the more likelihood there is of a traffic jam, or energy blockage. Practising the meditations in this book clears blockages at your junctions so that traffic can flow freely and uninterrupted along your energy highways.

"There are 72,000 nadis in this cage [the body]. Of these, the sushumna [the central nadi]
gives great delight to the yogis."
HATHA YOGA PRADIPIKA, 4.18

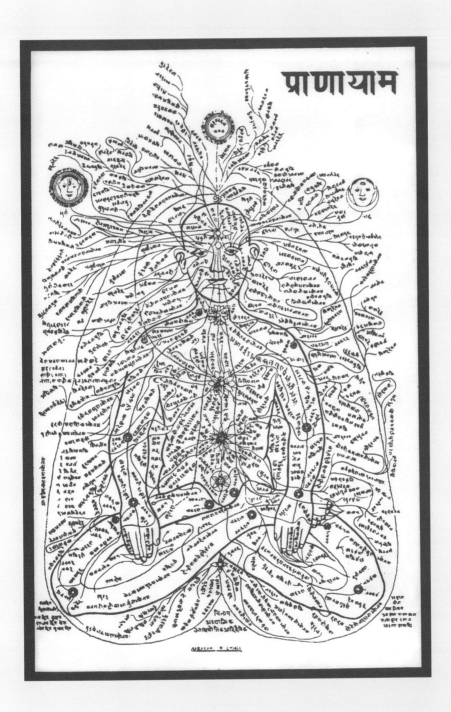

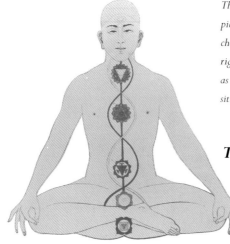

The three main nadi energy channels are traditionally pictured, as left, winding around each other. The ida channel begins on the left of the spine, the pingala on the right, and both twine around the central channel known as the sushumna, along which the seven major chakras are situated, pictured in the form of lotus flowers.

The three main nadis

Of the 72,000 nadis in your *pranamaya kosha*, the astral body's sheath of energy, only three are of relevance in our exploration of chakra meditation: the *ida* channel, which flows to the left of your spine; the *pingala* to the right; and the central channel that approximates your spine, the *sushumna*.

If you would like to experience the effect that your nadis have on your physical body, put down your book for a moment and hold the back of one hand beneath one of your nostrils. Exhale through your nose, then place the back of your hand under the other nostril. Exhale again. Notice how your breath feels a little stronger on one side. Repeat the experiment throughout the day; you will probably find that your "stronger" side changes every hour-and-a-half to two hours. Energetically, this reveals a normal change in predominance of the ida (left) or pingala (right) nadi – and of the corresponding hemisphere of your brain, because the right hemisphere controls the left side of your body and vice versa. As prana flows through these channels, it

"Wedged in between ida and pingala, the sushumna nadi carries six lotuses, endowed with six energies. These only the yogis know."
SIVA SAMHITA, 2.27

QUALITIES OF THE KEY NADIS

IDA	PINGALA
• **LEFT SIDE OF BODY**	• **RIGHT SIDE OF BODY**
• **RIGHT SIDE OF BRAIN**	• **LEFT SIDE OF BRAIN**
• *Symbolized by the moon and the goddess Shakti.*	• *Symbolized by the sun and the god Siva.*
• *Feminine*	• *Masculine*
• *Cool*	• *Warm*
• *Active*	• *Passive*
• *Yin*	• *Yang*
• *Calming*	• *Exciting*
• *Inward-directed*	• *Outward-directed*
• *Holistic*	• *Analytical*
• *Emotional*	• *Rational*
• *Subjective*	• *Objective*
• *Non-verbal*	• *Verbal*
• *Spatial*	• *Mathematical*
• *Simultaneous*	• *Sequential*
• *Intuitive*	• *Logical*

influences your behaviour and your mood in different ways: the key properties of the left and right nadis are set out in the chart above.

The only time that your breath flows evenly through both nostrils is during meditation, when your breath comes into the central energy channel, the sushumna. At this time, both sides of the brain are completely balanced, and the opposing but complementary qualities of mind listed in the chart above are united. This helps to restore balance in all spheres of life. Yoga breathing exercises are particularly helpful at dissolving energetic blockages in your nadis and bringing your breath into the sushumna, leading to a state of meditation in which your chakras open and function properly. One of the best is Alternate Nostril Breathing, which is demonstrated on pages 30–31.

PRELIMINARY BREATHING EXERCISE

It is a good idea to start each meditation in this book by practising *Anuloma Viloma* (Alternate Nostril Breathing). No other exercise purifies your nadis quite as quickly and thoroughly, or restores an equal flow of prana through the main energy channels as efficiently. Even if you are practised in meditation, it is useful to purify your nadis by performing at least ten rounds of this technique before you start meditating. As your nadis begin to be cleansed, over time, by your breathing exercises, meditation and yoga postures, you may find that you perspire a little more than usual. Invigorate your body still further by massaging this "magnetic energy" into your skin, and wait for at least 30 minutes before bathing or showering.

Positioning Your Hands

Fold your right index and middle fingers into your right palm to create the hand position used in this exercise, Vishnu Mudra. Hold your hand up, with your palm in front of your face. You will alternately use your thumb to depress your right nostril, and your ring finger and little finger to close your left nostril. Rest the back of your left hand on your left knee.

"When the nadis are full of impurities the breath does not go into the middle nadi, sushumna; then there is no arriving at the higher state of consciousness. When all the nadis, which are now full of impurities, become purified, only then can you successfully perform pranayama [control the prana]."
HATHA YOGA PRADIPIKA, 2.4–6

Alternate Nostril Breathing

---

1 *Sit in a comfortable meditation position, preferably with your legs crossed. Keep your back straight. Raise your right hand in Vishnu Mudra (see opposite) and depress your right nostril with your thumb. Breathe in through your left nostril for 4 seconds.*

2 *Also close your left nostril by depressing it with the ring finger of your right hand and little finger. Try to hold your breath without strain for 16 seconds.*

3 *Release your thumb from your right nostril, keeping your left nostril closed with your ring and little fingers. Breathe out through your right nostril for 8 seconds.*

4 *Keeping your left nostril closed, breathe in through your right nostril for 4 seconds.*

5 *Gently pinch both nostrils shut by replacing your thumb, and try to hold your breath for 16 seconds.*

6 *Release the fingers on your left nostril, keeping the right nostril closed with your thumb. Breathe out for 8 seconds. This exhalation completes one round of Alternate Nostril Breathing.*

7 *Build up to 10 rounds of this breathing practice daily, preferably before beginning any form of meditation.*

Easing the breath

If, at first, you find it difficult to hold your breath for 16 seconds, reduce the time, but keep the count in the ratio of 1:4:2. As you become more experienced, gradually increase the count, keeping to the same ratio. Do not try to hurry and do not strain to hold your breath.

AWAKENING KUNDALINI ENERGY

The ultimate aim of chakra meditation – once you are well versed in meditative techniques and have been working on them with a teacher for some time – is to channel the infinite spiritual potential that lies dormant within each of us up through each chakra in turn until it reaches your final, or crown chakra, and you experience absolute bliss. This vast well-spring of potential energy, known as *kundalini*, is regarded as a sleeping goddess, who takes the form of a serpent

THE EXPERIENCE OF AWAKENING KUNDALINI

- *Tingling in the spine, abdomen, neck and head.*
- *Sensation of a snake wriggling up the spine.*
- *Hot and/or ice-cold currents moving up and down the spine.*
- *Vibrations and feelings of restlessness in the arms, hands, legs and feet.*
- *Increased pulse and breathing rates.*
- *Hyper-sensitivity to sound, light and smells.*
- *"Seeing"(non-physical) lights or "hearing"anahata ("other worldly") sounds.*
- *Mystical experiences, cosmic glimpses, revelations, psychic or paranormal abilities.*
- *Craving for solitude.*
- *Gentle aches that move around the body but do not stress the joints or muscles.*
- *Stiffness in the neck, sometimes accompanied by a headache.*
- *Sleeplessness.*
- *Intense joy/bliss alternating with lower periods.*

"The Kundalini is described as being coiled like a serpent.Without a doubt, one that makes shakti [energy] flow [from the muladhara chakra upward] obtains liberation."
HATHA YOGA PRADIPIKA, 3.108

and lies coiled at the base of the spine. The goddess's name, Kundalini, derives from the Sanskrit *kundala*, which means "coiled" and signifies the vast potential power contained within a coil. The release of this coiled energy may be likened to the opening of the floodgates of a dam, which is why it is not something to pursue lightly. However, if you have been practising chakra meditation regularly, your nadis will be free from energy blockages and equipped with the strength to handle the increased load. Your energy body is also protected by three "circuit breakers" known as *granthi*, or knots, that do not allow large amounts of energy through until you are ready for a greater flow (see box below).

The movement through the nadis of such a high-voltage energy surge brings a heightened sensual, intellectual and spiritual awareness (common responses are detailed in the box opposite). Although the exercises in this book are unlikely to result in any uncomfortable sensations, if you are worried by any sensations or experiences, do consult an experienced meditation or yoga teacher.

PROTECTIVE KNOTS

In the "anatomy" of your astral body, three protective "knots" sit at three separate chakras to shield you from a premature or excessive release of kundalini energy along the sushumna nadi. Each knot, or granthi, *only opens to let released potential rise when the pranic layer of your astral body is ready to handle the flood of energy and when the nadis along which it would flow are clear and healthy.*

• BRAHMA GRANTHI, *in the root chakra, remains shut until you have overcome your attachment to stability, inertia and identification with the physical body alone.*

• VISHNU GRANTHI, *in the heart chakra, remains shut until you have overcome your attachment to action, ambition and passion, and forgive those who have wronged you.*

• RUDRA GRANTHI, *in the brow chakra, remains shut until you have overcome your attachment to your intellectual powers and your own self-image.*

chapter 1

MULADHARA CHAKRA

YOUR ROOT SUPPORT

Also known as the root chakra, the muladhara chakra is located around the base of your spine. This chakra is your energetic foundation — the Sanskrit word muladhara *translates as "root support" — and it helps you to find your path in life, to stand on your own two feet, to put down roots and to nourish yourself both physically and spiritually. At the muladhara chakra, you connect with the vehicle that carries you on your journey through life: your physical body.*

Purifying and balancing muladhara energy through meditation helps you to remain firmly rooted and develop a stable posture and steadiness of mind. By keeping in touch with your physical needs in this way, you equip yourself to function well on a day-to-day level as you develop your inner world and give life to creative and spiritual ideas.

Understanding
YOUR MULADHARA CHAKRA

The root chakra is associated with matter in its most dense form: its associated element is earth, the most solid of the elements. A limitless storehouse of potential spiritual energy, or *kundalini*, lies dormant in this chakra, held in place by the first of three psychic knots, *Brahma granthi* (see page 33). This knot keeps kundalini in the lower chakras by making you feel an intense craving for protection and security. Once you are strong enough to experience higher realms of consciousness, this knot of attachment unties so that prana can rise up your chakras.

When your root chakra is in balance, energy flows in two directions. The chakra releases energy downward, like a lightning rod, while at the same time drawing energy upward from the earth. As a result, you feel secure and safe. Life is stable, but filled with active, positive energy, and your patience and sense of community bring rewarding relationships.

If the energetic flow of your muladhara chakra is blocked, however, you might not feel as if you belong. You might feel disoriented and indecisive, not connect well with others, struggle with personal finance, jobs and relationships, and feel tired all the time. An over-concern with survival and security can manifest in a workaholic approach to your career and in difficulties in connecting with the spiritual side of life. Fear, prejudice, blind faith, hatred, intolerance, impatience and greed are other possible negative attributes of blocked muladhara energy.

If you experience such imbalances in your muladhara energy, it can be helpful to look back at trauma in your early life. Perhaps you were not nurtured as well as you could have been or felt that you did not "fit in" with your family or community. You may feel abandoned; perhaps

CHAKRA MEANING: *root support* ELEMENT: *earth* SOUND VIBRATION: *LAM*
SENSE ASSOCIATION: *smell*

you were adopted or suffered the loss of a parent or a parental divorce while young. Early trauma can amplify later upset, such as the break-up of a relationship, the loss of a job or a change in living conditions.

In the physical body, this chakra governs the immune and skeletal systems and the lower digestive tract. An imbalance in energy could manifest in chronic fatigue syndrome; IBS (Irritable Bowel Syndrome), constipation or haemorrhoids; obesity or weight issues; arthritis; foot, knee or leg problems; poor balance; and lower back pain or sciatica.

Emotionally, you may find yourself compensating for a lack of grounding by becoming too rigid to contemplate alternatives. If you are overly grounded you can find change difficult, too, and may become very controlling, or lacking in imagination and initiative. Working with this chakra helps to establish healthy grounding, as well as improving your energy levels, well-being and inner strength. The health of your root chakra sets the foundation on which all your other chakras rest.

WORKING WITH MULADHARA ENERGY

As you follow the meditations in this chapter, ask yourself the following questions. They can help you to see how you block your muladhara energy and to understand how you might rebalance it.

- *Do I need to reconnect with my body? How might I do this?*
- *Are my eating habits erratic? If so, how could I improve them?*
- *Am I successful at maintaining healthy, lasting relationships? If not, why not?*
- *Do I need to let go of relationships that have shown themselves to be unhealthy?*
- *Do I fully enjoy giving and receiving, and see life as a healthy exchange of energy?*
- *Do I allow myself to become "stuck" in unhelpful ways of thinking and behaving?*
- *How can I be more decisive when I feel "weak-kneed"? (The minor chakras in the knees are governed by muladhara energy.)*
- *Am I prepared to embrace positive change? If not, how could I be better prepared?*

Meditating on a Yantra:
TUNING INTO YOUR ROOT CHAKRA

Meditating on the root chakra's image, or *yantra* (see right), while reciting its mantra, rebalances mind and body by linking the visual (right) and verbal (left) hemispheres of your brain. After a few days' practice, try to feel manipura energy in your spine (see bottom right).

Yantra Meditation

1 *Cover a low table with a clean cloth, then prop up the* yantra *illustrated opposite on top, so that it is slightly below eye level when you are seated. Light a candle and some incense (see page 47).*

2 *Sit comfortably upright, preferably cross-legged with your back straight (see page 16). Take 10–20 deep breaths; let your breath settle.*

3 *With half-closed eyes, gaze at the yantra's four crimson petals. Start at the upper right-hand petal and slowly rotate your eyes clockwise.*

4 *After several rotations, take your gaze to the yellow square, the symbol of earth energy. Move your eyes clockwise over its corners, which represent the four corners of the Earth and the four directions.*

5 *Next, focus on the black elephant, sign of strength, grounding and your fundamental needs for survival. He is associated with the Hindu god Ganesha, remover of obstacles and guardian of this chakra.*

6 *Bring your attention to the Sanskrit character. This reads as* LAM, *mantra of the earth element. Say it silently as you gaze at its form.*

7 *Look at the downward-pointing triangle in the centre of the square. It shows the downward-moving nature of muladhara energy. Its angles represent the starting point of your three main nadi energy channels.*

8 *Lastly, take your gaze to the coiled snake representing the limitless potential energy lying dormant in this chakra. After meditating for at least 20 minutes, open your eyes. Repeat the meditation daily.*

Progressing further

When the yantra is so familiar that you can visualize it without looking at it, sit in a meditative position with your spine straight, close your eyes and take your focus to the base of your spine. Visualize the yantra above as a pattern of energy here. Feel its rays of energy spreading outward and hear the mantra LAM. Sit in meditation for at least 30 minutes.

Meditating on the Elements:
THE EARTH ELEMENT

The element associated with the muladhara chakra — earth — encompasses not just the rocks and terrain of our planet, but all solid matter. In the yogic tradition, *vibhuti*, holy ash, is placed on the forehead to remind wearers that the body will return to this element, a sentiment echoed in the words of the funeral service in the *Book of Common Prayer*: "earth to earth, ashes to ashes, dust to dust". Meditating on the element earth increases your sense of stillness, stability and groundedness. Feeling well-rooted in the present creates a firm foundation for spiritual practice, and the meditation opposite helps you to establish such a solid base.

Before you start the exercise, it is helpful to place items on a home altar that physically connect you with the earth: soil brought back from holy lands, stones, pine cones and seeds, a magnet, a compass or even pieces of interesting metal. In the Tibetan tradition, a metal object known as a *vajra*, or thunderbolt, is held in the hand during meditation to represent the grounding properties of a lightning rod.

As part of the meditation opposite, you repeat affirmations: positive suggestions stated consciously with the intention of changing negative thought patterns into more beneficial ones. Use any suggested affirmations that seem applicable, or substitute personal examples.

"Visualize the quintessence of earth. Its symbol is a yellow square bearing the mantra LAM *as its secret seed. Place the image of this four-petalled lotus in the heart while restraining the prana and mind for two and a half hours. By the practice of this meditation, one conquers the element earth; no solid objects can injure the practitioner; the practice causes steadiness."*
GHERANDA SAMHITA, 3.70

Earth Meditation

1 *Kneel in front of your altar (see opposite) with your knees and feet together, buttocks resting on your heels, and palms on your thighs (see below). If you prefer, you can sit cross-legged, or on a chair with your bare feet flat on the ground.*

2 *Now place the backs of your hands on your knees or thighs and make Prithivi (Earth) Mudra by joining your ring fingers with their respective thumbs (see left).*

3 *Close your eyes and become aware of the effects of gravity on your body. Begin to experience a pleasant heaviness that becomes a feeling of stability and stillness. Then think about the qualities of the element earth. Feel as if you are rooting yourself firmly, while drawing up stability and strength from the ground beneath you.*

4 *Mentally repeat an affirmation, such as:*
"My life is firm and grounded."
"My patience is infinite."
"I stand up for what I believe in."
"I have my feet planted firmly on the ground."
"My path in life reveals itself to me."
"I am exactly where I need to be."
"I am nurtured by the energy of the earth."

5 *Spend at least 30 minutes on the practice, then stretch your legs.*

Chakras and the Emotions:
OVERCOMING FEAR

If your muladhara energy is not steady and balanced, thoughts of loss may disturb your inner peace, sap your vitality and drain your reserves of energy. The visualization opposite helps you to transcend fear, the key negative emotion associated with an imbalance in the root chakra.

Fear doesn't always manifest as a phobia, or even as overt anxiety, shyness or dread (for example, of public criticism or illness). Many of us experience fear more as an absence of security or as an ungrounded restlessness. This could be in response to an event that has threatened your survival or may be the result of worrying about losing a possession or person.

The image of a sturdy tree, such as an oak, offers an ideal focus to help you to get in touch with your inner strength and conquer fear. The picture helps to ground you in time and space, bringing deep calm and the assurance that you have the resources to survive any experience.

The visualization opposite is best practised outdoors: in a park, a forest or your own garden. If possible, sit beneath or near a majestic tree, preferably an oak or banyan tree. Alternatively, sit in a quiet place and visualize the strong, thick roots of a massive tree growing deep into the earth. Feel reassured that, however hard the wind may blow, this tree can never topple.

"He whose mind is not shaken by adversity, who is free from attachment, fear and anger, is called a sage of steady mind."
BHAGAVAD GITA, II.56

Oak Tree Visualization

---

1 *Sit in a comfortable meditation position, preferably cross-legged. Hold your head up tall, lengthen your spine and let the back of your neck reach upward, while the rest of your body remains steady and relaxed.*

2 *Visualize an oak tree and ponder its qualities: strength, endurance, stability, deep-rootedness and an ability to draw up nourishment.*

3 *Then, to release old self-images and to inspire new ways of being to emerge, mentally repeat affirmations based on the qualities of the tree:*

"I have the strength to endure the upheavals of life."

"I am grounded and secure."

"I embody courage."

"I draw sustenance from the world around me."

4 *Sit silently with these thoughts for at least 20 minutes. Before getting up, mentally thank the tree. A simple thought of gratitude enhances your ability to tune into nature on a deep level.*

INTERPRETING THE VISUALIZATION

Spiritual practice becomes simpler if you can conquer fear and insecurity, but the roots of fear run deep, so it is not advisable to attack it directly. The more we struggle, the more fearful we often become, so instead of dwelling on any fears that arise during the Oak Tree Visualization, try to think of their opposites. Most people find that the positive thoughts engendered overcome the negative ones.

As you absorb the qualities of the tree, take care that your strength does not become harsh and inflexible. Oak trees appear to be more vulnerable than other types of tree to being struck and split apart by lightning: an apt analogy for the results of a strength that resists the flow of life. To counterbalance rigidity in thought and action, it is useful also to cultivate flexibility, a focus of the meditations in chapter 2 (see pages 52–67).

Samanu:
CLEANSING VISUALIZATION

Try this four-part meditation when you feel in need of grounding and to cleanse your nadis (see pages 28–29). Before you start, sit comfortably with your legs crossed. Join the tips of your left thumb and index finger, then rest the inside of your wrist on your left knee, fingers pointing downward (see left). This hand position, Jnana Mudra, steadies your mind and grounds energy. Then raise your right hand and fold the two fingers beside the thumb into your palm. This is Vishnu Mudra (see below). In this exercise it allows you to use your right thumb to close your right nostril; and your right ring and little fingers to close your left nostril.

Purifying with the Air Element

1 *With your right hand in Vishnu Mudra, close your right nostril by pressing it with your right thumb (see below left). Inhale through your left nostril, mentally saying the mantra of air,* YAM, *until you have filled your lungs. All the time fix your attention on your heart chakra, the energy centre of the air element. Picture air or wind flowing through the nadis, blowing away impurities.*

2 *As you finish the in-breath, pinch both nostrils shut by pressing the left nostril with your little and ring fingers. Retain your breath for a few seconds as you say* YAM. *Focus on your heart.*

3 *Release the thumb from your right nostril. Exhale very slowly through the right nostril while you repeat* YAM, *focusing on your heart chakra.*

Purifying with the Fire Element

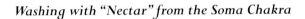

4 *Keeping your left nostril closed, inhale through your right nostril (see right) while you silently say* RAM, *the mantra of fire. Fix your attention on the solar-plexus chakra and visualize fire burning away impurities.*

5 *Press with your thumb to close both nostrils and hold your breath for a few seconds, saying* RAM *silently.*

6 *Release your left nostril. Exhale slowly through the left nostril as you repeat* RAM *mentally. Keep your focus on your solar-plexus chakra.*

Washing with "Nectar" from the Soma Chakra

7 *Inhale through your left nostril while you silently say* TAM, *the moon mantra. Focus on the minor soma chakra above your palate and behind the inner arch of your left eyebrow (see page 138).*

8 *Press with your ring and little fingers to close both nostrils and hold your breath for a few seconds, saying* TAM. *Imagine "nectar" cleansing away any remaining impurities from your nadis and soothing them.*

Grounding with the Earth Element

9 *Release your right nostril and exhale through it very slowly. As you exhale, mentally say* LAM, *the earth mantra. Feel the sound ground you. Then, take your attention to the chakra at the base of your spine.*

10 *Release both nostrils and bring your right hand into Jnana Mudra to match your left hand, resting the wrist on your right knee. Sit silently for at least 10 minutes, focusing on the base chakra and repeating the mantra* LAM. *Feel secure, present and connected with the earth.*

Tools for Working with
MULADHARA ENERGY

Drawn from healing therapies, the following "tools" can enhance the benefits of meditating on the muladhara chakra. Experiment to see which ones suit you best, thinking of them as supplements to (not a substitute for) meditation. If you are pregnant or have a medical condition, consult a medical practitioner before using essential oils.

Flower essences

Place 4 drops under your tongue (or take in water) before meditation.

• **BEECH** assists you in shedding intolerant attitudes.

• **CLEMATIS** grounds you in the present when you dream of the future.

• **LOOSESTRIFE** helps you to release buried emotions and old fears.

• **ROCK WATER** loosens a rigid frame of mind.

• **CHERRY PLUM** helps you to let go while remaining grounded.

• **WILD OAT** supports you if you feel unsure of your direction in life.

Essential oils

For a pre-meditation bath, blend 3–5 drops of essential oil into 1 tsp jojoba, sweet almond or olive carrier oil and pour into running water as you fill the bath. Alternatively, use as directed below.

• **PATCHOULI** evokes feelings of warmth, security and being "earthed".

• **SANDALWOOD** is beneficial if you feel "stuck"; brings fresh vision.

• **VETIVER** helps you to seize chances and make life-changing decisions.

• **GINGER** helps you to stand your ground; lifts apathy and indecision.

• **THYME** boosts your immune system: blend 2 drops thyme oil and 5 drops lavender oil in 1 tbsp olive oil as bath oil. (*Use* Thymus vulgaris.)

"To be healthy, one needs the earth and the sky."
CHINESE PROVERB

• **BASIL** reduces debilitating nervousness, stress symptoms, loss of smell and extreme mental fatigue. (*Never use directly on your skin.*)

• **CLARY SAGE** cheers you when you feel run down and overwhelmed by life; good for depression. (*May cause drowsiness; avoid alcohol.*)

Crystals, gems and stones

Gemstones act as energy amplifiers when placed in contact with your chakras. Wear them in jewelry, place them on the base of your spine or simply hold the precious stones in your hand before meditation.

• **HEMATITE** offers stress-resistance; works as a protective shield.

• **SMOKY QUARTZ** brings present focus; dissolves emotional blocks.

• **BERYL** helps you to let go of fear and the past, and get on with life.

• **BLACK TOURMALINE** protects, calms and expels fear; best set in silver.

• **GARNET** counters illusions; acts against depression; beats insecurity.

Incense

• **CEDAR**, **SAGE** and **PATCHOULI** aromas increase the effectiveness of any of the meditations in this chapter. Incense is especially appropriate because the muladhara chakra's associated sense is smell.

Grounding foods

Eat organic foods (choose those grown in earth) to prevent you from feeling "spaced out". Avoid overindulging as excess muladhara energy brings a sluggish heaviness. Good grounding foods include:

• **ROOT VEGETABLES:** beetroot, burdock, carrots, parsnips, potatoes, sweet potatoes, turnips, yams.

• **VEGETABLE PROTEIN:** beans, legumes, dairy produce, nuts, nut butters, tofu and soy products.

• **SEEDS:** pumpkin seeds, pine nuts, sesame and sunflower seeds and the oils sourced from these seeds.

YOGA ASANAS FOR MULADHARA ENERGY

Add the poses shown here to your regular practice or use them as a pre-meditation tune-in. They help you to draw up earth energy, as do *Bhaddhakonasana* (Cobbler Pose), *Vatayanasana* (Horse Pose) and *Tadasana* (Mountain Pose), which are not shown. Indian dancing, *Haka* (Maori dance), walking and jogging also boost root chakra energy.

MULABANDHA

Sitting cross-legged, contract your anal muscles, lift your pelvic floor and draw your tailbone inward and up. Imagine pulling prana (energy) forcefully upward. When you feel confident, practise this while you perform yoga postures and breathing exercises, as well as during meditation, to boost your strength and to help energy to surge upward.

Ardho-mukha-shwanasana: Downward Dog Pose

1 *Begin on all fours, placing your hands beneath your shoulders and your knees directly beneath your hips.*

2 *Tuck your toes under and slowly straighten your knees, lifting your hips toward the ceiling and pushing backward. Also press back with your calves so that your heels come as close to the floor as possible. If your heels reach the floor very easily, move both feet back a pace. Hold the posture for at least 1 minute.*

Vrikshasana: Tree Pose

1 *Stand with your feet together and arms by your sides, spreading your body weight evenly over both feet. Bend your right knee and place the sole of your right foot on the inside of your left thigh (lower if you're less flexible). Keeping your left leg straight and steady, bring your palms together at your chest. Fix your gaze on a point on the ground about 1m (3ft) in front of you.*
2 *Slowly straighten your arms and lift them over your head, keeping your palms together.*
3 *Hold the position for 30–60 seconds, picturing your left foot sending roots into the ground. Do not resist gravity: let it help you to root firmly. Repeat on other side.*

Utkatasana: Chair Pose

1 *Stand with your feet about 15cm (6in) apart and parallel. Look at a point directly in front of you. Extend your arms forward from your shoulders, keeping them parallel to the floor with your palms facing downward.*
2 *Anchoring your heels to the ground, bend your knees and tuck your bottom under, as if you are sitting on an invisible chair placed behind you.*
3 *Hold for at least 30–60 seconds.*

Minor Chakras:
AWAKENING YOUR FEET

Located in the arch of each foot is a minor chakra considered part of the muladhara chakra. Known as the plantar chakra, it consists of primary grounding points that transmit prana between your energy system and the earth. When "tuned", it helps you to turn your thoughts into acts.

An imbalanced plantar chakra can make you feel ungrounded, out of balance (literally and metaphysically), "spaced out" and emotionally numb. Being clumsy or accident-prone are other strong indicators that your plantar chakras may not be functioning fully. Awakening the plantar chakra is especially useful if you spend too much time thinking or worrying, or feel unconnected to your body and those around you.

To restore plantar energy balance you might try reflexology or walking barefoot on grass or on a beach. Or you could use the Walking Meditation opposite, either alone or with a group of people. Whether you choose to walk in a line or a circle, be aware of each step and of the ground beneath you. Reflect on earth, the element of the root chakra.

VARIATIONS ON THE PRACTICE

Takefumi, the Japanese practice of walking barefoot over bamboo, formed part of the training of samurai warriors to enhance vigour and grounding. Replicate this process by walking over PVC piping laid to create a path. If you have a pebble path, try the Chinese art of "stone stepping": simply walk barefoot over pebbles for 30 minutes each morning.

"As a single footstep will not make a path on the earth, so a single thought will not make a pathway in the mind. To make a deep physical path, we walk again and again. To make a deep mental path, we must think over and over the kind of thoughts we wish to dominate our lives."
HENRY DAVID THOREAU, *WALDEN*

Walking Meditation

---

1 *Choose a peaceful spot outside and stand barefoot on the ground. If you are walking with others, measure an arm's length between each person, and maintain this distance throughout the meditation.*

2 *To ground yourself, place your feet parallel and hip-width apart, and distribute your body weight evenly over both feet.*

3 *Close your eyes halfway. Fix your gaze approximately $^1/_2$m (2ft) in front of your feet. Place your left hand on top of your right hand at waist level, palms facing upward to receive inspirational energy. Take a few deep breaths.*

4 *Step your right foot forward by about 15cm (6in). Take a moment to ground yourself, then step your left foot forward by the same amount. Ground yourself again (see step 2), then move your right foot forward, as before, setting up a slow, rhythmic walking motion. As you continue to move forward in this way, maintain your focus on each step.*

5 *Tune each step with your breath. Inhale as you lift your foot. Exhale as you place it back on the ground. Notice how a natural rhythm develops.*

6 *As you walk, centre your weight over the mid-line of your body; do not allow it to shift forward or hang back. Feel each foot rooting deeply.*

7 *Observe how your body is involved in the action. See how each knee bends, lifts and straightens. Be aware of your moving ankles, hips, spine and shoulders. Keep bringing your attention back to the soles of your feet and their meaningful interaction with the earth.*

8 *If desired, silently repeat the earth mantra LAM each time you inhale and each time you exhale. Practise the meditation for as long as feels right before returning to your regular activity.*

chapter 2

SWADHISTHANA CHAKRA

THE SEAT OF YOUR CREATIVITY

The second chakra, located around the kidney and genital region of your body, is known as the swadhisthana, or sacral, chakra. This chakra governs the energy of creativity, pleasure, sex, procreation, control and morality. It also presides over dreams, fantasies and emotions.

The Sanskrit word swadhisthana has many connotations. It is translated as "the sacred home of the self", "the sweet place" and "the goddess' favourite standing place". In chapter 1, we saw how the function of the base chakra (stability and grounding) is symbolized by a square or cube. The sacral chakra is best expressed as a circle or sphere. Although less stable, this shape is more free and open to change. The meditations in this chapter help you to create an increased sense of flexibility and flow in your life.

Understanding
YOUR SWADHISTHANA CHAKRA

The qualities of water (swadhisthana's associated element) epitomize this chakra's nature: liquid, flowing, flexible and adaptive. Water also has cleansing and purifying properties, which is appropriate, because when this chakra's energy becomes unbalanced or blocked, it creates the feeling of having done something wrong or shameful.

The sacral chakra is associated, too, with the sense of taste, and the taste symbolism of everyday conversation hints at its energy. When you wish someone "sweet" dreams, relate a "bitter" memory or bemoan a "soured" relationship, you enter the world of the swadhisthana chakra.

When the swadhisthana chakra is open and balanced, you blossom as a person: you are sensitive, intuitive, idealistic, and full of dreams, plans and healthy desires (creative impulses originate at your sacral chakra). You are adaptable, accept change and can go with the flow.

However, going too far down this route throws the energy of the sacral chakra off balance, resulting in constant flux, an inability to ground yourself or set boundaries, and a tendency to become over-emotional or highly theatrical. You might spend too much time daydreaming or attach too much importance to gratifying sensual tastes. The butterfly flitting from flower to flower and the fish that allows itself to be caught through greed symbolize such imbalances.

If your sacral chakra is blocked or unbalanced, it becomes difficult to taste life's sweetness: nothing seems good enough, and depression can ensue. You may feel as if you have no choice, no ability to change and no initiative. Creatively, you may suffer from a type of writer's block. Some people with an unbalanced sacral chakra seem over-emotional;

CHAKRA MEANING: *sacred home of the self* ELEMENT: *water*
SOUND VIBRATION: *VAM* SENSE ASSOCIATION: *taste*

others become insensitive to their own emotional needs and those of others, and may be unable to express feelings. In extreme cases, this can even lead to aggression. Sometimes people become manipulative and prone to false displays of emotion, such as "crocodile tears", to get their way. Blocked or imbalanced sacral-chakra energy can also bring denial of pleasure and fear of sex, and can manifest in unyielding, self-imposed boundaries, including extreme yoga practice.

Physically, the sacral chakra governs the body's liquid elements: blood, lymph, mucus, semen, urine and saliva. It is the seat of kidney energy (regarded in Chinese medicine as the basic vigour of life) and maintains the kidneys, bladder, urinary, reproductive and circulatory systems. Health issues associated with blocked swadhisthana energy include hardening of the arteries, varicose veins, anaemia, kidney and bladder problems, menstrual ailments, impotence and frigidity.

Contrary to popular ideas, opening the sacral chakra is not about enhancing sexuality. Achieving balance means directing sexual energy so that it becomes a force of awareness. Opening this chakra is more about letting go of guilt and frustration, and enjoying the flow of life.

WORKING WITH SWADHISTHANA ENERGY

As you use the meditations in this chapter, ask the following questions. They highlight ways to unblock swadhisthana energy.

- *Am I open to positive change? How can I make myself more so?*
- *Am I greedy for sensation or experience? How can I enjoy life better without becoming addicted to its pleasures?*
- *Is my outlook on life overly emotional, or too negative?*
- *How can I become more fearless without becoming reckless? What self-imposed fears or anxieties can I begin to overcome today?*
- *If I feel swamped (a sign of excessive swadhisthana energy), how can I ground myself?*

Meditating on a Yantra:
TUNING INTO YOUR SACRAL CHAKRA

Daily meditation on the sacral-chakra image or *yantra* (see right) enhances your ability to put your creative energies to best use. Alongside regular yoga practice, it augments your physical and mental flexibility. Once you can visualize the yantra, try the progression (see bottom right).

Yantra Meditation

1 *Cover a low table with a clean cloth, then prop up the chakra illustration opposite on top, so that it is slightly below eye level when you are seated. Light a candle and some incense (see page 65) and place a vase of fresh flowers on the table.*

2 *Sit comfortably upright, preferably cross-legged with your back straight (see page 16). Take 10–20 deep breaths, then let your breathing settle into a slow, natural rhythm.*

3 *With eyes half closed, gaze at the outer edge of the picture. Look at the deep-red coloured lotus. Rotate your eyes clockwise around its six petals, which represent this chakra's pattern of radiant energy.*

4 *Slowly move your eyes inward, to the white crescent shape. This represents the moon that controls the tides and water, the element of the swadhisthana chakra.*

5 *Next look at the animal, or carrier of the chakra: a* makara, *or mythological crocodile with a snake's tail. In Indian tradition, he is associated with Ganga, the personification of the river Ganges.*

6 *Bring your attention to the Sanskrit character. This reads as* VAM, *the* bija, *or seed, sound of the swadhistana chakra. Silently say or softly whisper the mantra to enhance your inner tuning.*

7 *After meditating for at least 20 minutes, gently open your eyes. Repeat the meditation daily to attune yourself to swadhisthana energy.*

Progressing further

When the yantra is so familiar that you can visualize it without looking at it, sit with your spine straight, close your eyes and focus on the base of your spine. Apply Mulabandha (see page 48) or visualize roots growing into the earth. Once you feel rooted, draw your focus upward, to your sacrum. Visualize the yantra above as an energy pattern here, feel its six rays of energy emanating outward and hear the mantra VAM. Sit for 30 minutes or more.

Meditating on the Elements:
THE WATER ELEMENT

The liquid nature of our planet and our bodies is epitomized by the element associated with the swadhisthana chakra – water. By practising the Water Meditation opposite, you become able to tune into the flexible and fluid energy of this element. In doing so, you gain the ability to accept that change is a fact of life and you learn to truly appreciate the gift of going with the flow.

"Visualize the quintessence of water as a divine nectar which is white like a jasmine flower or a conch shell. Its form is circular like the moon. Fix the consciousness on the water element; it will destroy all sorrows and remove excess heat from the body. Water cannot injure the person who practises this meditation. He will never be in danger of drowning, even in the deepest ocean."
GHERANDA SAMHITA, 3.72–74

Before beginning the meditation below, cover a low table with a cloth and place on it items that connect you physically and energetically with the element water. They might include sea shells, pieces of coral, willow branches or parts of other plants with watery energy. If desired, place a bowl of water on your meditation table, which can often help you to express any "drowned", or subjugated, thoughts or emotions. If you feel as if you have lost touch with your dreams or find yourself over-stimulated by (or cut off from) your feelings, you will probably find that this meditation is of great value.

Next prepare yourself by taking a relaxing shower or bath. Do not add oil or bubbles to the bath water; instead, focus on the experience of being in the water. If possible, submerge yourself in an ocean, stream or lake, or take a dip in a swimming pool. Drink a large glass of water just before starting to meditate, and feel it flowing through your body.

Water Meditation

1 *Sit in front of the table (see above) in a comfortable meditative position, preferably with your legs crossed. Keep your back straight.*

2 *Resting the backs of your hands on your knees or thighs, join the tips of your little fingers and thumbs in Varun (Water) Mudra (see right). Relax your other fingers.*

3 *Close your eyes and think of the qualities of water. Feel as if you are as fluid as liquid.*

4 *Mentally repeat an affirmation, such as:*
   "I trust myself to follow my dreams."
   "I adapt with grace to any situation."
   "I release ideas that are no longer useful."

5 *Spend 30 minutes or more on the exercise, then open your eyes and stretch your legs.*

Chakras and the Emotions:
TRANSCENDING GUILT

When your swadhisthana chakra is closed or its energy falls out of balance, you may feel overcome by guilt – even if there is no apparent reason. This emotion can manifest as a feeling of shame about your body, as sexual inhibition or as an emotional disconnection from other people. Rather than allowing yourself to "drown" in such feelings of guilt and the sorrow that they bring, try the Lotus Visualization opposite.

Although each of the chakras is symbolized by a lotus flower, the swadhisthana chakra has a particularly intimate connection with this beautiful plant. The lotus is primarily a water plant: it thrives in the element of the swadhisthana chakra. The plant is rooted in mud, and yet the flower never becomes muddied. Its home is water, but it never gets wet. Its nature is fluid and flowing, but it is adamant in its resolve to grow upward, toward the light. And so from the sludge rises the world's most beautiful bloom.

Eastern philosophers often use the example of water when contemplating the nature of the human soul. Yogis explain that the soul is ever-pure; it can never be impure. Like water, it can carry impurities, but these pollutants can never change the basic nature of the soul. Think about these ideas for a few minutes before you begin the Lotus Visualization opposite.

"Be careful what you water your dreams with. Water them with worry and fear and they will produce weeds that choke the life from your dream. Water them with optimism and solutions and you will cultivate success."
LAO TZU, TAO TE CHING

Lotus Visualization

1 *Place a picture of a lotus (or of any flower) on a low table and sit in a comfortable meditation position in front of it. Look intently at the petals until you can close your eyes, but still "see" the flower.*

2 *See this flower as an analogy of your life. Just as a flower is unsullied by the mud out of which it grows, do not allow any negativity in which you are rooted to affect you. Just as a flower strives to reach the light, go with the flow of your environment and know what your goals are. Like the lotus that stands in water but is not wet, exist in the world without letting yourself be tarnished by it.*

3 *If any negative thoughts arise during this meditation, try not to dwell on them. Instead, see them as bubbles rising to the surface of the water around the lotus, and watch them burst one by one. If you do not identify with the thoughts, they cease to exist. Meditate for at least 20 minutes before gently opening your eyes.*

INTERPRETING THE VISUALIZATION

The Lotus Visualization stimulates a gradual emotional cleansing of your sacral chakra. If you practise it on a regular basis, you will find that your swadhisthana energy becomes more balanced and the chakra itself begins to open. However, be warned that you may experience a range of sexual feelings or imagery as you meditate on this chakra. Feelings of guilt, lust, betrayal and jealousy are the shadow side of the swadhisthana chakra, and, taken to an extreme, may manifest as troubling images.

Do not let any such images or thoughts upset you: allowing repressed feelings to come to the surface is evidence that your swadhisthana energy is manifesting in a positive way. And along with the surprising or even disturbing thoughts will come the strength to overcome them. By rising above any negative images or thoughts you set yourself free to taste all the goodness life has to offer.

Learning to
GO WITH THE FLOW

The moon is a powerfully resonant symbol of the swadhisthana chakra that reminds us of the importance of change. Its symbolism is especially empowering if you feel the need to let go of past issues that are hindering your growth, and if you need to accept change and transition. As you let go of the familiar, safe and secure (muladhara energy), you free yourself to travel to unknown places and learn to value swadhisthana energy for itself, not for what it brings.

The Moon-energy Meditation opposite helps you to go with the flow and is best practised somewhere outside with a good view of the moon. If this is not possible, gaze at the moon through a window as you meditate, or cover a low table with a clean cloth and prop up a picture of the moon on top so that it is slightly below eye level when you are seated in front of the table. This image of the moon then becomes your point of focus for the meditation.

This exercise becomes most effective if you practise it every night throughout an entire lunar cycle – from one new moon to the next new moon. It is best to meditate just before going to bed in the evening, for at least 30 minutes, surrendering to the eternal wisdom that urges you to let your life flow – and grow – organically.

"*Within the swadhisthana is the white, shining, watery region in the shape of a half-moon, and therein, seated on a makara is the seed mantra* VAM, *pure and white as the autumnal moon.*"
SAT-CHAKRA-NIRUPANA, 15

Moon-energy Meditation

---

1 *Sit comfortably, with your back straight, in a place where you have a good view of the moon. Gaze at it for a few moments and try to feel its gentle energy flow into your swadhisthana chakra.*

2 *Now close your eyes and imagine that you are at a crossroads where as many roads as you can visualize converge. Think about how the crossroads represents a coming-together of all your hopes and dreams.*

3 *Ask your subconscious to direct your swadhisthana energy to the right path in life for you. Trust that you will go with the flow of your destiny, just as the ebb and flow of the tides are influenced by the moon.*

4 *Ask yourself, "Which path will I choose?" or "If I could see my future, what would it bring?", whichever question feels more relevant to you. Will your subconscious guide your swadhisthana energy up the chakra system, so that it merges with the power of your manipura (solar-plexus) chakra on the path to the heart? Or will it turn your swadhisthana energy away from the spiritual path of the chakras altogether, and instead direct it along a more materialistic road? Consider as many possible paths as you wish.*

5 *Continue the meditation for at least 30 minutes. Then, before you go to sleep, place a small notebook and pen next to your bed to use as a dream diary. Your dreams may bring insights that help you to determine which path you should follow.*

6 *In the morning when you wake up, write down your first thoughts or whatever you remember of your dreams.*

7 *After a month or so, carefully read through your dream diary and look out for any recurrent messages or themes. Are they encouraging you to steer your life in a certain direction? Do they answer the question you posed about your future?*

Tools for Working with
SWADHISTHANA ENERGY

Use any of the following healing "tools" to support your meditation on your swadhisthana chakra. They will help you to let go of past ways of being and explore new paths. If you are pregnant or have a medical condition, consult a medical practitioner before using essential oils or herbal teas.

Flower essences

To overcome the negative emotions that can surface when you work with this chakra, place 4 drops of flower essence beneath your tongue (or sip them in water) before beginning to meditate.

• CLEMATIS brings focus; stops meditation becoming a dreamy escape.
• EASTER LILY allows you to integrate your sexuality and spirituality.
• FAWN LILY lets you share your spiritual gifts and stop hiding away.
• WALNUT dispels illusions that bind you to the past; aids path-finding.
• PINE helps you to overcome guilt as you take responsibility for life.
• WILLOW helps to banish self-pity and bitterness about adversity.

Essential oils

A pre-meditation bath washes away energy that may be blocking your spiritual flow. Blend 3–5 drops of essential oil into 1 tsp jojoba, sweet almond or olive carrier oil. Pour it into running water as you fill the bath.

• FRANKINCENSE zaps growth-blocking energy; brings tranquil insight.
• PATCHOULI deters dreamy meditation; brings you well into the body.

"Nothing in the world is more flexible and yielding than water. Yet when it attacks the firm and the strong, none can withstand it, because they have no way to change it. So the flexible overcome the adamant, the yielding overcome the forceful."
LAO TZU, *TAO TE CHING*

• **Jasmine** links the creativity of swadhisthana to the chakras associated with love (your heart chakra) and spirituality (your crown chakra).

• **Clary sage** is linked with the sacred, timeless state Indigenous Australians call "Dreamtime". (*Oil may cause drowsiness; avoid alcohol.*)

• **Sweet marjoram** lifts guilt; aids celibacy. (*Use* Origanum marjorana.)

• **Cypress** helps you to move on after a major life change, such as a career move or the death of a loved one. (*Replace oil every 6 months.*)

Crystals, gems and stones

Wear as jewelry, place by the chakra or simply hold before meditating.

• **Coral** helps you to balance emotions and to maintain enthusiasm.

• **Garnet** brings about a balanced energy field around your body.

• **Moonstone** aids intuition; calms the emotions; brings objectivity.

• **Pearl** absorbs extraneous thoughts that detract from meditation.

• **Aquamarine** attunes spiritual awareness; for journeys over water.

• **Carnelian** brings initiative; overcomes apathy and writer's block.

• **Citrine** releases emotional stagnancy that builds at the sacral chakra; for more potency, anoint the stone with 1–2 drops of patchouli oil.

• **Clear quartz** brings the wisdom and stability to see a higher self.

Incense

• **Cedarwood** and **juniper** cleanse guilt and so increase the effectiveness of any of the meditations in this chapter, especially if burnt together.

Freeing foods

Water, herb teas and juices of the foods below help the kidneys to cleanse the physical body and balance the subtle body's water element.

• **Sweet fruits:** apples, pears, peaches, apricots, melons, mangoes, oranges, pomegranates, strawberries, raisins, currants, figs.

• **Vegetables:** watercress, lettuce, spinach, cucumbers, tomatoes.

YOGA ASANAS FOR SWADHISTHANA ENERGY

Support your swadhisthana energy by including the poses shown here in your regular yoga sessions. Alternatively, practise them as a pre-meditation warm-up. Other helpful postures include *Sethu Bandhasana* (Bridge Pose), *Janu Sirshasan* (Forward Bend with One Leg Bent), *Upavishta Konasana* (Seated Angle Pose) and *Chandrasana* (Crescent Moon Pose). Swimming and hula dancing are also beneficial.

Yoga Mudra: Energy Seal

1 *If you can, sit in* Padmasana, *Lotus Pose, with feet resting on your opposite thighs (see below left). If not, kneel in* Vajrasana *by bringing your knees and feet together, and resting your buttocks on your heels.*

2 *Make your hands into fists and place one on each crease where your thigh connects to the trunk of your body.*

3 *Inhale deeply. As you exhale, bring your forehead toward the floor (see below right). Breathe deeply as you hold the pose for 10–30 seconds, feeling your fists stimulating sacral-chakra energy. Then relax.*

Kaliasana: Goddess Squat

1 *Stand with your feet wider than shoulder-width apart and turn your toes out at a 45-degree angle.*
2 *Bend your knees and squat down, making sure that your knees remain positioned over your feet. Bring your palms together at your chest, using your elbows to push your knees outward. Hold the pose for 30–60 seconds before slowly standing up.*

Matsyasana: Fish Pose

1 *Lie flat on your back with your legs and feet together. Place your hands, palms downward, beneath your thighs, one on each side.*
2 *Bend your elbows and lift your chest as high as possible, then gently take your head back until your crown rests on the ground. Keep your weight mainly on your hands. Avoid pressurizing your head or neck.*
3 *To take advantage of your wide-open chest, breathe as deeply as possible. Engage your rib-cage in the action by picturing each side as the gills of a fish, opening to pull oxygen and prana into your body.*
4 *Hold the position for 30 seconds, then come down and relax on your back.*

chapter 3

MANIPURA CHAKRA

YOUR POWER BASE

Progressing up through the chakra system, we reach the third major chakra, the manipura chakra, at the solar plexus. Although it is referred to as the navel centre, most of us sense its energy between the navel and the base of the sternum.

This is the body's stronghold — its fortress. Literally translated, the Sanskrit word manipura means "city of shining jewels", and it is here that you store your most precious asset: your sense of self. The manipura chakra is related to willpower and self-esteem. From here stems your ability to set strong yet flexible personal boundaries, to act and to adjust: all change and personal growth begins at this level. The way in which you use the energy of this chakra manifests in your ability to change yourself and your situation in life. "Transformation" is the key word related to the manipura chakra and it is therefore the focus of the meditations in this chapter.

Understanding
YOUR MANIPURA CHAKRA

While your two lowest chakras govern physical and emotional survival, the energy at your manipura chakra is more transformative, having the potential to bring about change and growth. The energy of the element fire has its seat at this chakra. Fire changes all it touches, converting matter (the visible elements earth and water of the lower chakras) into heat and gases (the invisible elements of the higher chakras).

The manipura chakra is associated with our sense of sight; indeed, fire in the form of light allows us to see. But at this chakra, seeing and being "seen" signify more than physical sensation: they represent a human need to be acknowledged as a unique individual.

When the energy of your solar-plexus chakra is balanced and unblocked, you feel unique, valued, confident and energetic. People respond to your charisma and respect your integrity (this chakra relates to personal honour). They sense your power and know you have the strength to keep secrets, yet are not secretive by nature. You are spontaneous, open and loving – your energy moves freely up to the heart chakra. And because your channels down to the first two chakras are open, you feel grounded and go with the flow. Your strong sense of personal worth equips you to avoid excess and to respect boundaries, and so although you enjoy challenge, you are not a workaholic.

An imbalance in manipura energy often brings with it a need to manipulate or to be controlled by others. If you have overabundant manipura energy you may lack sensitivity, "burn out" and not tolerate those with less energy. This is the realm of the judgmental, aggressive perfectionist with an overbearing interest in self-aggrandizement and

> **CHAKRA MEANING:** *city of shining jewels* **ELEMENT:** *fire*
> **SOUND VIBRATION:** RAM **SENSE ASSOCIATION:** *sight*

the source of the desire for name and fame. As well as vanity and pride, an imbalance of energy at this chakra can lead to hatred and anger (whether expressed or not). Under-activity in the solar-plexus centre may be the source of emotional neediness as well as attention-seeking. If you lack inner fire, you may also lack the energy to put ideas into practice and fear rejection, which can lead to indecisiveness, over-sensitivity to criticism, poor self-confidence and self-image, and even to depression. You may feel like a victim: people who lack in protective strength often become vulnerable to others' thoughts and feelings.

In your physical body, the solar plexus is the seat of your digestive fire: it controls your digestive organs (including the pancreas and liver) and muscles, and acts as your inner thermostat. An energy imbalance is often linked with digestive complaints, food intolerance, blood sugar problems, diabetes and eating disorders, paralysis and muscle spasms.

Working with your energy flow at this chakra stokes the "fire in your belly" and helps you to put thoughts and dreams into action.

WORKING WITH MANIPURA ENERGY

As you work through the meditations in this chapter, ask yourself these questions. They can help you to see how you block your manipura energy and to understand how you might rebalance it.

• *Am I ruled by doubt and fear? How can I transform this into positive energy?*

• *Am I the kind of person who has trouble making decisions? When I finally decide on a course of action, do I lack the energy to carry it through?*

• *Do I feel a need to be right in every discussion?*

• *Am I emotionally needy? Do I always have to be the centre of attention?*

• *Do I lack willpower? Do I compensate by being a "control freak"?*

• *Do I allow other people's opinions to control my life? How can I stop this without becoming emotionally rigid or overly aggressive?*

Meditating on a Yantra:
TUNING INTO YOUR
SOLAR-PLEXUS CHAKRA

In the meditation below you focus on this chakra's image or *yantra* (see right). This abstract visualization leads to a deep state of meditation and helps to open your manipura chakra so that energy ascends up your chakra system. It's important to begin by purifying yourself with the cleansing exercise on pages 44–45.

Yantra Meditation

1 *Cover a low table with a clean cloth, then prop up the chakra illustration opposite on top, so that it is slightly below eye level when you are seated. Light a candle and some incense (see page 83).*

2 *Sit comfortably upright, preferably cross-legged with your back straight (see page 16). Take 10–20 deep breaths; let your breath settle.*

3 *With half-closed eyes, gaze at one of the ten blue petals that represent this chakra's energy pattern. Slowly rotate your eyes clockwise around the petals. Imagine that the blue is the most luminous part of a flame.*

4 *After some time, shift your gaze to the downward-pointing triangle that symbolizes the element fire. It is the colour of the rising sun. Think of this chakra as the seat of your own "fire": your life-force and charisma. Note the "foot", or entrance, on each side of the red triangle.*

5 *Next, focus on the ram. Consider his strength, stamina and ability to charge head on. He is the vehicle of Agni, Hindu god of fire.*

6 *Let your eyes find the Sanskrit character. It reads as RAM, the seed mantra of this chakra. Repeat it mentally as you gaze at its form.*

7 *Continue meditating for at least 20 minutes. By doing so you are asking the gatekeeper of the manipura chakra to open the door and allow your energy to ascend to the heart chakra. Repeat every day.*

Progressing further

When the yantra is so familiar that you can visualize it without looking at it, sit with
your spine straight, close your eyes and take your attention to the base of your spine. Apply
Mulabandha (see page 48). When you feel rooted, draw your attention to your sacral region,
then your solar plexus. Feel the yantra as a pattern of energy here, sensing its rays of energy
moving like flames and its mantra RAM radiating out. Meditate for at least 30 minutes.

Meditating on the Elements:
THE FIRE ELEMENT

Your solar-plexus energy centre is the source of your imagination, your vision of the future and your desire for action. It is here that you come to terms with the past and "burn" accumulated *karma* (the consequences of your past actions). Fire, the element of the manipura chakra, is used creatively in the meditation opposite to transform negative qualities into positive ones with its purifying properties.

Meditation on the manipura chakra in the presence of fire is thought to give you the power to command with authority, and to organize, lead and manage successfully. It is also reputed to promote immunity, leading to good health and a long, productive life.

You may like to practise the Fire Meditation opposite in front of an open fire. Alternatively, cover a low table with a cloth and place items on it that physically connect you with the element fire. You will need some candles (for safety, place them on a very large metal tray or piece of slate), and you might also like to place a vase of marigolds or sunflowers in your meditation space. Before you start the meditation, place a pen and paper close to hand.

"Manipura chakra is as radiant and bright as the sun dominating the dawn. The prana is to be drawn in and held here while the mind meditates on the fire element for two hours. This meditation dispels the deeply ingrained terror of death. Fire can never injure the one who practises this meditation."
GHERANDA SAMHITA, 3.75

Fire Meditation

1 *Sit in front of a fire or your chosen candles (see left) in a comfortable position, preferably with crossed legs. Make sure your back is straight.*

2 *Close your fists, releasing the thumbs. Rest your hands on your knees with thumbs pointing straight up in Agni (Fire) Mudra (see right).*

3 *Mentally bathe in the warmth and power of the fire or candles. Think of a past unpleasant experience or relationship.*

4 *Write this memory on a piece of paper. Key words will suffice. Carefully hold one corner of the paper to the fire and let the flames "eat" it. Drop the paper safely onto the fire or metal tray and watch it burn to ashes. Feel freed from the memory.*

5 *Next, think of a current experience that is not going well. Decide what you would like to do: steer it in a certain direction? Let go of it? Write your plan on a piece of paper and let the flame burn it, as before. Let the fire give you the energy to put your plan into action.*

6 *Think of your visions for the future. Write down one you hold dear. Hold it to the flame as before. Let the fire show you how to transform your vision into reality (in India, fire is the messenger of the gods).*

7 *End by mentally repeating an affirmation, such as:*
   "I offer up my negative qualities to the fire of transformation."
   "My enthusiasm empowers me to achieve great things."
"I claim my own power and accept responsibility for every part of my life."
   "My healthy appetite for adventure equips me to enjoy challenges."
   "My relationships are filled with courage, openness and confidence."

8 *After 30 minutes or more, blow out the candles or extinguish the fire.*

Chakras and the Emotions:
UNDERSTANDING ANGER

Anger, rage, bitterness and resentment are expressions of an imbalance or blockage of energy at the fiery-red manipura chakra. These negative emotions are stored energetically in the solar-plexus region, often for years, whether you anger easily, are only irritated by small things or stoically resist any external expression of rage. The Indian scripture *Chandipath* salutes "the goddess who appears in all beings in the form of anger". She has the gift of alchemy, being able to transform ego-based energy into spiritual power. The aim of the meditation opposite is to absorb some of that transformative energy, to enable you to turn the red rage of anger into the rosy glow of the new dawn.

You can practise this meditation at any time of day and in any place, perhaps while performing simple manual tasks, such as gardening, chopping vegetables or walking. But do turn off the television, radio or music. Give your hands to the work and your mind to the meditation.

"Anger's my meat; I sup upon myself,
And so shall starve with feeding."
WILLIAM SHAKESPEARE, *CORIOLANUS*

Meditation to Find the Causes of Anger

---

1 *Begin by remembering an incident in which you became angry or felt irritated. For example, you may have been late for an appointment and unable to find a place to park. Just as you found a parking space, another driver grabbed the spot.*

2 *Ask yourself, "Why did I get angry?". Try to identify both the stimulus of your anger and its underlying cause. For example, the answer, "Because he took my parking place" is the trigger for the anger rather than its underlying reason (which may concern the nature of the appointment or your state of mind at the time).*

3 *Contemplate whether it is what people do that makes you angry, or whether it is your own evaluation of the situation. To help you, imagine sitting on a bus when, suddenly, someone's hands cover your eyes. Would you feel angry or frightened? How would your perception change if you turned around to recognize a friend you hadn't seen for years? Would you still feel angry?*

4 *Holding these examples in mind, vow to analyze everyday sources of anger or irritation each time they arise, so that when you feel the first symptoms, you will ask yourself, "Why am I really getting angry?".*

INTERPRETING THE MEDITATION

The meditation above is not intended to stifle your anger, to instruct you in ways of calming down, nor to encourage you simply to accept negative experiences. Its purpose is simply to help you to identify and then transform the inner causes of your anger. As you practise it over the following days and weeks, notice how sensations of anger and irritation start to melt away as you no longer get carried away by those emotions. Most people find that their anger is replaced by a feeling of empathy: an energetic connection to other people at the solar-plexus chakra.

Sensory Meditation:
TRANSFORMATIVE EATING

Although we eat several times a day, most of us rarely concentrate on the tastes, smells and sensations of eating. We focus instead on television or chatter with friends; we let our minds wander to work or family matters, or we simply hurry to finish our food. This leads to an imbalance in the energy of the manipura chakra.

As well as being the centre of your body's transformational energy, the manipura chakra is the seat of your body's digestive fire. Its job is to "digest" and assimilate whatever comes in, whether that be food or ideas. Without this conversion, your body, mind and emotions are unable to absorb essential nourishment.

The Eating Meditation opposite puts you in touch with this energy and also connects you in a very physical way to the ingredients of life. Try not to think of it as meditating while eating. Rather, feel that the act of eating itself becomes a form of meditation that links you with an ancient spiritual practice: eating as a meditation is ritualized in many religions, from the taking of the Eucharist in Christianity to *prasad* in Hinduism (which transforms food into divine essence). It is best to practise this form of meditation in the morning when your taste buds are still fresh.

"The process of eating is divine; the food itself is divine; the person who is eating is divine. Therefore eating is a process by which the eater makes a sacred offering to the divine. And the fire which consumes the offering (digestion) is also divine. Thus by seeing the divine everywhere in action, one reaches that divine state."
BHAGAVAD GITA, IV. 24

Eating Meditation

1 Prepare a plate containing three pieces of fruit with different textures, for example a slice of pineapple or citrus fruit, some ripe banana, and sweet grapes or crisp apple. Don't just choose fruits you enjoy — it is interesting to include some that you find less tasty. Switch off distractions, such as the television or background music.

2 Centre yourself by breathing deeply into your abdomen. Use your breath to connect you to the source of your hunger in the pit of your stomach — the manipura chakra.

3 Look at the first piece of fruit, observing its colour, shape and texture. Then pick it up, enjoying its tactile qualities.

4 Close your eyes and take the fruit to your lips. Notice how the smell of the fruit and the action of touching it to your lips begins to stimulate energy at your solar plexus.

5 Bite into the fruit; notice whether it is crunchy or soft. If the taste is pleasant, follow the enjoyable sensations throughout your body. If it is a taste you like less, observe any waves of tension.

6 Now chew slowly, resisting the urge to swallow. Notice an immediate change in the intensity of the flavour. Observe the effect that chewing has on your solar plexus. Chew each bite 20–30 times, pausing occasionally to take a few deep breaths. As you swallow, feel the food moving down your oesophagus into your stomach.

7 Finally, visualize the fruit being digested and assimilated. Mentally see the energy of the solar-plexus chakra distributing nutrients to various parts of the body. Repeat steps 3–7 with the remaining fruit.

8 Try to repeat this meditation every day for 40 days. Vary the foods you use: as well as fresh fruit, try dry or savoury snacks, such as olives, raisins and even potato chips from time to time.

Meditation in Motion:
SPINNING INTO STILLNESS

Your manipura chakra is the gravitational centre of your body, and the Whirling Meditation that follows shows how to become more centred in it through movement. As you spin in the meditation, you are impelled beyond your limitations – beyond dizziness, nausea and fear of losing control – to a self-confident abandonment in a simple movement.

Spinning to free yourself from the chatter of the mind produces a powerful juxtaposition: from external energetic movement comes a profound inner stillness.

Practise the Whirling Meditation at any time of day or night, ideally on a grassy lawn or in a room free from furniture. Don't eat or drink for three hours before whirling, have bare feet and wear loose cotton clothing.

Whirling Meditation

1 *Stand with your feet slightly apart, crossing your arms over your chest. Place your right hand on your left shoulder and your left hand on your right shoulder. Make sure your left arm is on top.*

2 *Close your eyes and take a few breaths, breathing deeply into your solar plexus. Return to this centred position while whirling if you feel dizzy at any time.*

" 'Tis light makes colour visible. At night
red, green, and russet vanish from your sight,
So too, light by darkness is made known,
all hidden things by their contraries are shown."
RUMI, *MATHNAWI*

3 *Half open your eyes and gaze at the ground. Slowly unfurl your arms, using the momentum to begin an anticlockwise rotation of your body that starts at your torso and extends down into your legs. Move from right to left, making the solar plexus your pivot point.*

4 *Extend both arms straight out from your shoulders with your left palm facing upward and your right palm turned down. Visualize energy from above entering your raised palm, passing across your shoulders and flowing down through your other palm into the earth.*

5 *Keep your left foot grounded as your pivot point. And use your right foot to drive the rotational movement by taking short, staccato steps (keep them slow and rhythmic, like the hammer of a blacksmith).*

6 *Gradually build up speed. As the whirling takes over, you may experience your body as a whirlpool of energy.*

7 *As you spin, keep bringing your awareness back to your solar plexus to maintain your balance, but don't worry if you topple over. Keep your body relaxed so that you will land softly even if you fall. Then let the earth absorb your energy. Lie on your abdomen for a few moments, with your solar plexus in contact with the earth. Then stand up and resume the whirling.*

8 *At first, whirl for 1 minute. With practise, build up to 15 minutes, and finally even an hour's session.*

9 *When you have finished whirling, come back to the centred starting position (see left), with your arms crossed at your chest. Then sit observing your still mind and the sense of power in your solar plexus.*

Tools for Working with
MANIPURA ENERGY

The following therapeutic tools support your manipura chakra as you begin to harness your will and realize ambitions. Many help to purify your emotions (essential because your solar plexus is the seat of power, and power tends to corrupt). If you are pregnant or have a medical condition, consult a medical practitioner before using essential oils.

Flower essences

Taking flower essences before meditation helps you to overcome negative emotions that might surface when you are working with manipura energy. Place 4 drops beneath your tongue (or sip in water).
• MIMULUS comforts the manipura chakra to ease anxiety.
• BUTTERCUP brightens dark thoughts, boosts confidence, nurtures self-sufficiency; helps you to recognize talents that need to come to light.
• IMPATIENS calms impatience and irritability; helps you to deepen your life experience without experiencing burn-out.
• ROSE OF SHARON helps to transmute vibrations of anger; gradually releases the tension that may build when emotions aren't expressed.

Essential oils

For a purifying pre-meditation bath, blend 3–5 drops of essential oil into 1 tsp jojoba, sweet almond or olive carrier oil and pour into running water as you run the bath. Alternatively, use as stated.
• CHAMOMILE eases expectation and tension that can build at your solar plexus as a result of frustration; promotes a "sunny" disposition.
• BERGAMOT helps you to release stagnant energy. (*Use FCF grade.*)

"One who meditates on the Manipura lotus is constantly happy."
SIVA SAMHITA, 5.81

• JUNIPER soothes if you feel uncomfortable or frightened; removes pre-meditation negativity. Blend 5 drops in 1 tsp olive oil as a bath oil.

• FENNEL acts as a spiritual shield. Burn 1 drop in an oil diffuser if you feel vulnerable meditating. For an energy-lifting bath oil, blend 2 drops each of fennel, caraway, orange and marjoram oils in 1 tbsp olive oil.

• PEPPERMINT brings manipura energy into balance; calms excessive pride and the inferiority it can mask; enables transition and transformation.

Crystals, gems and stones

Wear in jewelry, place by the chakra or just hold before meditation.

• ADVENTURINE QUARTZ balances manipura energy; boosts well-being.

• TOPAZ opens and balances; encourages confidence and change.

• YELLOW CITRINE boosts self-confidence; allows you to access personal power; place on the solar plexus to unblock stagnant energy.

• BLUE SAPPHIRE soothes anger; anoint with 1 drop chamomile oil.

• GREEN JADE helps to align your manipura and anahata chakras.

• RUBY improves digestion; develops your will in a positive direction.

Incense

• SANDALWOOD tones and nurtures manipura energy.

• NAG CHAMPA calms and fosters meditation.

• DRAGON'S BLOOD RESIN amplifies protective energy and consecrates a space energy. Place on charcoal to burn.

Nurturing foods

The following spices build inner fire – the seeds cool excess fire, and the carbohydrates are supportive:

• SPICES: black pepper, cayenne, cloves, ginger.

• SEEDS: fennel, anise, cumin, linseed (flax seed), sunflower seeds.

• COMPLEX CARBOHYDRATES: rice, oats, millet, pasta, bread, muesli.

YOGA ASANAS FOR MANIPURA ENERGY

To balance manipura energy, use the following poses in a yoga session or before sitting to meditate. To stimulate energy further, practise the meditations in this chapter in the kneeling pose *Vajrasana* (see page 41). Also try jogging, belly dancing, hula-hooping and sit-ups.

Parivritta Trikonasana: Rotated Triangle Pose (a)

1 *Stand with your feet approximately 1m (3ft) apart. Stretch your arms straight out to the sides at shoulder height. Turn your left foot in a little and then turn your right foot out at a 90-degree angle.*

2 *Rotate your upper body to face right and place your left hand on the outer side of your right foot (or a yoga block). Stretch your right arm up and look up at your hand. Hold for 1 minute. Repeat to the left.*

Ardha-matyendrasana: Half Spinal Twist (b)

1 *Sit on your heels. Drop your hips to the left side of your feet. Bring your right foot flat to the floor on the outer side of your left knee.*

2 *Stretch your left arm up and take it around your right knee; aim eventually to hold your right ankle with your left hand. Place your right hand behind your right hip and look over your right shoulder. Hold for 30–60 seconds. Repeat to the other side.*

Parivritta Utkatasana: Awkward Twist (c)

1 *Stand with your feet and knees together. Bend at your knees and hips, as if to sit on a chair. Turn your chest to face left.*

2 *Bring your palms together at your chest. Press your right elbow against the outside of your left knee. Look up. Repeat, turning your chest right.*

UDDHYANA BANDHA

Uddhyana Bandha is the manipura chakra's most important practice. Stand with your feet a little more than hip-width apart. Bend your knees slightly and rest your hands on your thighs. Inhale deeply through your nose and exhale forcefully through your mouth. When your lungs are completely empty, draw your diaphragm up, toward your throat. Hold for as long as you feel comfortable, then release and take a deep breath.

(a)

(b)

(c)

chapter 4

ANAHATA CHAKRA

YOUR HEART CENTRE

Your heart chakra is the most complex and talked-about of chakras. Lying at the energetic centre of your subtle body, it links your physical and spiritual realms. The heart centre transforms higher energy from the upper chakras into baser substance, so that it can move down the chakras and manifest on a physical level. At the same time, it converts solid energy from the lower chakras into subtler form, so that this energy can move up and appear as ideas, thoughts and inspiration.

The Sanskrit word anahata *literally translates as "un-struck". This chakra is said to produce intangible astral harmonies when it is "touched" — plucked or struck like a musical instrument. The key purpose of this chapter is to encourage you to reach out and touch others, and, in turn, to allow yourself to be touched by the joys of life.*

Understanding
YOUR ANAHATA CHAKRA

As we progress up the chakra system to the heart chakra, we encounter the first of our major energy centres to be associated with an invisible element: air, or everything that is gaseous in form (neither liquid nor solid). This includes prana, the non-physical energy we draw in with every breath, often referred to as "vital air" or life-force, which also has its seat here. Anahata chakra is the home, too, of the "winds" of change, which have the power to sweep away or evaporate the negative emotions of the lower chakras, such as fear, guilt, shame and anger.

When the energy of the heart chakra is flowing well, you feel grounded in the lower chakras, yet "free as a bird". You are self-accepting, trusting, compassionate, forgiving, filled with hope and emotionally empowered. As touch is the sense associated with the anahata chakra, you are also well equipped to reach out to others and to allow people and experiences to "touch" you. The impulse to touch begins at the heart, and your ability to love may be regarded (both physically and metaphorically) as an openness to being "touched". Although the concept of the chakra system is Indian, healers from many traditions work with the heart centre as well as with touch, because a healthy heart chakra ensures deep and lasting healing – "love conquers all".

Your heart chakra plays a vital role in transforming ideas into physical reality and vice versa. Given that thoughts and events are not always positive, the heart chakra can cause unpleasant experiences to forge negative thought patterns, and even transmute negative thoughts into physical ailments. If the flow at your heart chakra is over-active, your energy can become too "airy" and dispersed. You might find it

> **CHAKRA MEANING:** *un-struck* **ELEMENT:** *air* **SOUND VIBRATION:** YAM
> **SENSE ASSOCIATION:** *touch*

WORKING WITH ANAHATA ENERGY

As you follow the meditations in this chapter, ask yourself these questions. They can help you to see how you are blocking your anahata energy and to understand how you might rebalance it.

• *Do I express my emotions openly and from the heart? If not, why not?*

• *Do I look to others to fulfil my emotional needs? If yes, why might this be?*

• *How can I initiate deep and heartfelt healing in my life?*

• *How do I include others in that healing process?*

• *Do I have any negative attachments? If so, how could I let go of them?*

• *Do I hold onto grief? If so, how can I begin to let go of this?*

hard to come down to earth and you are likely to feel lonely, isolated and afraid of being hurt. If, on the other hand, your anahata energy is under-active, you might feel "heavy" and lacking in joy, or be possessive, clinging, jealous or selfish. People with an unbalanced heart chakra often feel emotionally unfulfilled, self-conscious or even anti-social.

In your physical body, anahata energy governs your heart and lungs. When it becomes unbalanced, ailments can include asthma, pneumonia or chronic bronchitis; upper-back or shoulder pain; and even lung or breast cancer. A "broken heart" is a sign that your heart chakra has shut down. Divorce, death, abuse, abandonment or betrayal can all cause this type of emotional numbness, as your heart chakra barricades itself from unendurable pain, cutting off communication with the other chakras and, as a result, leaving you feeling empty: filled only with air.

As you awaken your heart chakra through meditation, notice how you develop a heart-felt strength that protects you from negativity and brings increased sensitivity to the energies of others as well as love for yourself. Forgiveness, compassion and unconditional love are essential if you are to open this chakra to allow your energy to ascend upward.

Meditating on a Yantra:
TUNING INTO YOUR HEART CHAKRA

By meditating on the heart chakra's image or *yantra* (see right), you sense how this chakra forms the body's energetic point of balance. Feel the symmetry between heart and head, masculine and feminine, and material and spiritual desires as you do the exercise below.

Yantra Meditation

1 *Cover a low table with a clean cloth, then prop up the chakra illustration opposite on top, so that it is slightly below eye level when you are seated. Light a candle and some incense (see page 99).*

2 *Sit comfortably upright, preferably cross-legged with your back straight (see page 16). Take 10–20 deep breaths; let your breath settle.*

3 *With half-closed eyes, gaze at the top outer edge of the picture. Slowly rotate your eyes clockwise around the 12 deep-red petals that show the chakra's radiant energy. Imprint the image on your mind and heart.*

4 *Moving inward, look at the six-pointed star, the shape associated with the anahata element, air. Observe its smoky colour. Connect the six points to the directions up, down; back, forward; right and left. See how the star's triangles intersect. The upward-pointing triangle represents Siva, or passive, masculine energy. The downward-pointing triangle stands for Shakti: active, creative feminine energy.*

5 *Look at the jumping deer, always on the move. He leaps with delight, as does your joyous heart. But, in Indian legend, he is infatuated by his own scent and runs restlessly in search of it. Do you, too, find yourself chasing worldly desires when happiness lies in your heart?*

6 *Now gaze at the Sanskrit character, which reads as* YAM, *mantra of the element air. Silently repeat it to untie any emotional knots and to let energy rise to the higher chakras. Continue for 20 minutes daily.*

Progressing further

When the yantra is so familiar that you can visualize it without looking at it, sit with your spine straight, close your eyes and take your attention to your heart centre. Visualize the yantra above as an energy pattern within your chest, its 12 rays of brilliant energy and its mantra YAM radiating outward. Practise for 30 minutes or longer.

Meditating on the Elements:
THE AIR ELEMENT

If you are feeling stifled or suffocated by life, it may be time for a "change of air". Freeing up your energy at your heart chakra by following the Air Meditation opposite is like taking a breath of fresh air. It allows you to experience life with fewer mental limitations, and those who practise it regularly tend to become more confident and full of hope. Meditating on the element air also helps to develop your inner beauty and personal magnetism by making your mind and body feel much lighter and more carefree.

As with some of the other "element" meditations, the exercise opposite is best practised outside, or at least near an open window. Sit in a garden or throw open the doors and windows of your meditation space. Feel the breeze on your skin and hear the wind rustling the leaves on the trees. To enhance this meditation, hang some wind chimes nearby: their sounds will increase your awareness of the movement of the element associated with this chakra, air.

"The quintessence of air is to be visualized as a glowing speck of smoky grey, symbolized by the mantra YAM. Here the prana should be united and the mind held in concentration for two hours. This air meditation makes it possible to float and walk on air. One who practises this meditation never dies as the result of any aerial disturbance. This is a very powerful practice ..."
GHERANDA SAMHITA, 3, 77–79

Air Meditation

1 *Sit comfortably in a meditative position, with your legs crossed and back straight.*

2 *If you feel too burdened and need to shed emotional weight, place your hands in Prana Mudra (see right) by joining the tips of each thumb to the ends of your ring and little fingers. Rest the backs of your hands on your knees with your palms facing upward.*

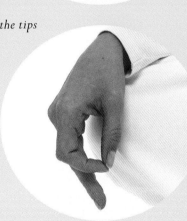

If you feel too "airy", adopt the grounding Jnana Mudra (see below right) by joining the tips of your thumbs and index fingers. Rest the insides of your wrists on your knees with your fingers pointing downward.

3 *Ask yourself the following questions:*
   "Do I keep old relationships hanging in the air? Do I need to release them?"
   "Do I let emotional wounds control me?"
   "For what do I need to forgive myself?"
   "Who must I forgive in order to be free?"

4 *Make an affirmation that expresses the air of change you need in words, such as:*
   "I forgive myself and release all feelings of guilt and hurt."
   "I forgive ... and am grateful for the lesson that he/she taught me."
   "My heart is weightless and free of unnecessary burden."
   "I know great joy and therefore have great energy."
   "My feet are firmly rooted, and my spirit is boundless like the air."

5 *Silently repeat the affirmation from the heart for at least 20 minutes.*

Chakras and the Emotions:
UNRAVELLING GRIEF

Grief is the negative state of an overly "airy" heart chakra. Whether the cause is a death, an illness or a broken relationship, grief is experienced by most of us as a feeling of emptiness in the chest cavity. As the love centre of your energetic system, your heart chakra needs to be freed from such emotional negativity before healing can take place.

The heart chakra is the seat of *Vishnu granthi*, an energetic knot of grief, pain and spiritual limitations (see page 33). Until you "untie" this knot and let go of grief and inner wounds, your spiritual energy is blocked from soaring upward to your higher chakras, and your innovative energy is prevented from flowing downward through your creative centres. The visualization opposite helps you to untie knots. If you have pets, you might wish to have them in the room with you during this meditation. Animals seem to know instinctively how to let go of pain; they are great teachers of unconditional love. It is probably best not to practise with young children around. They tend to request attention and may inhibit you from expressing emotions.

INTERPRETING THE VISUALIZATION

If you are finding it hard to emotionally disconnect from people who have hurt you, it can help to know that letting go does not absolve these people from the future consequences of their actions: karma will win out. Once you let go of this hurt, it will be replaced by a sense of the inter-relatedness of all life. This is a sign that your anahata chakra is opening, allowing you to experience the compassion that is your natural state of being.

"His love was like the liberal air, embracing all, to cheer and bless."
WILLIAM WINTER, *I.H. BROMLEY*

Untying Knots Visualization

---

1 *Sit in a warm, quiet room, preferably in a cosy, padded chair. Light some candles. Take off your shoes and make yourself comfortable.*

2 *Close your eyes and visualize your heart as a jumbled mass of threads that represent your emotions. As you look closely, become aware of those threads that represent negative feelings, such as old hurts you are still holding onto or grief that you have been unable to express.*

3 *Check whether some of the threads are now attached to people who have passed out of your life, to experiences that are now over, or to objects that once caused you pain, but no longer do. If your "heart strings" are still attached to these people, experiences or objects, decide to disengage yourself from them.*

4 *Picture yourself untying the knots, one by one, and letting go of their painful memories. Notice as you work on one knot how other threads occasionally become looser and then begin to unravel. Some threads may not even require you to untie them at all; they may start to fall away of their own accord.*

5 *As the knots release, feel yourself becoming more relaxed: sense that you are mentally and physically less "tied up in knots". In place of the previous tangle, you may begin to see a more simple, positive pattern emerging in your heart.*

6 *Repeat this visualization as many times as is useful. Come back to it whenever you feel particularly tense, tied up in knots or grief-bound.*

Metta:

OPENING YOUR HEART

The rose has strong symbolic connections with the heart chakra. In the West, the rose is considered to be the most beautiful of flowers: a symbol of completion, perfection, the mystic centre and representative of the heart itself. The Rose Meditation below is very similar to one of the most important Buddhist meditation practices, known as *metta*, or "loving-kindness". Metta meditation opens your heart, develops concentration and helps to introduce you to your "heart of hearts". If you practice the simple but potentially powerful meditation on a regular basis, you may experience a healing of past traumas and an emotional release similar to that brought about by metta meditation.

Rose Meditation

1 *Place a rose in front of you on a low table covered with a cloth, and sit silently in front of it in a comfortable meditative position, preferably with your legs crossed and your back straight. After taking a few deep breaths, allow your breathing to settle.*

2 *Gaze at the rose and inhale its fragrance for a moment. Then start to study the arrangement of its petals, noticing how they spiral out from the centre of the flower. For a few minutes reflect on the symbolism of the rose and how it stands for continuous, unconditional love.*

3 *Close your eyes and bring your awareness to the centre of your chest. Visualize an unopened rosebud lying there. Watch intently as the bud slowly opens, noticing how each petal unfolds to create a spiral pattern. Allow yourself to be in awe of its beauty, fragrance and colour.*

"The rose speaks of love silently, in a language known only to the heart."
ANONYMOUS

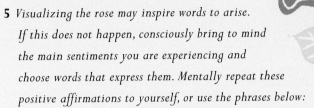

4 *As the flower opens within you, feel your*
heart centre opening, too. Notice how the
healing warmth radiating from your heart
creates well-being throughout your body.

5 *Visualizing the rose may inspire words to arise.*
If this does not happen, consciously bring to mind
the main sentiments you are experiencing and
choose words that express them. Mentally repeat these
positive affirmations to yourself, or use the phrases below:

> *"May I be happy."*
> *"May I be healthy."*
> *"May I live with ease."*
> *"May I be free of dis-ease."*

Practise the meditation only to this point for the first few days,
dwelling on steps 1–5 for 20 minutes or longer.

6 *After several days, continue beyond steps 1–5 by incorporating steps*
6–9. Visualize the face of someone you care about, such as a friend
or family member and direct the phrases of loving kindness to them:
"May … be happy. May … be healthy," and so on.

7 *Then call to mind someone who you know is going through a*
paricularly difficult period. Imagine the warmth of your heart
radiating out to this person. Mentally repeat the same phrases for
them: "May … be happy. May … be healthy," and so on.

8 *Finally, think of someone you feel has injured you or who you dislike.*
Feel your heart communicating compassion to that person. Mentally
repeat the phrases: "May … be happy. May … be healthy," and so on.

9 *As your heart chakra starts to open, memories of past hurt(s) may*
come to mind. Be nurturing with yourself. You may wish to end the
meditation by repeating the Sanskrit mantra, Lokah samasta sukhino
bhavantu, *meaning "May all beings everywhere be happy and free."*

Tools for Working with
ANAHATA ENERGY

The following tools support you as you work to open your heart centre, fostering devotion, compassion and clarity. It is important to "check in" daily on your heart chakra by recording your emotions and concerns in a journal. If you are pregnant or have a medical condition, consult a medical practitioner before using essential oils or herbs.

Flower essences

Place 4 drops under your tongue (or take in water) before meditating.

• CALIFORNIA WILD ROSE helps you to give of yourself wholeheartedly.

• CHICORY guides misdirected loving energy; eases a desire to control.

• HEATHER increases insight if you are consumed by your own problems; lets you access personal suffering when extending compassion to others.

• HOLLY expands your heart chakra; teaches acceptance and universal love; breaks down imagined boundaries that make you feel separate.

• WATER VIOLET helps you to open up and speak from your heart.

Essential oils

For a pre-meditation bath blend 3–5 drops essential oil into 1 tsp sweet almond or olive carrier oil; pour into running water, as you fill the bath.

• ORANGE BLOSSOM OR NEROLI relieves emotional exhaustion; helps to strengthen any frayed links between your heart and your mind.

• ROSE enhances compassion and comfort during times of sorrow; helps to link your heart with the minor chakra in the palms of your hands.

• BERGAMOT re-opens your heart chakra if grief has closed it; boosts joy; instils the courage to use your talents. (*Use FCF grade.*)

"By steady focus on the heart chakra, a full understanding of the nature of the mind is gained."
PATANJALI, *YOGA SUTRAS*, 3.34

• **JASMINE** helps your heart chakra to balance the energies of the higher and lower chakras; stimulates self-worth; links you to the spiritual.

• **LILAC OIL BLEND** assists forgiveness; helps you to recapture the innocence and sweetness of youth (but only when you are ready).

• **LAVENDER** encourages emotional balance, grounding you in your physical body; facilitates your connection with the spiritual realm.

• **ROSEMARY** links you with divine feminine energy that opens your heart and boosts faith; helps you to recall lost loved ones without grief.

Crystals, gems and stones
Wear in jewelry, place near the chakra or just hold before meditation.

• **ROSE QUARTZ (ROSELLE)** aids compassion; anoint with 1 drop rose oil.

• **BOJI STONE** brings joy and a powerfully healing energy to meditation.

• **MALACHITE** unblocks energy flow to your heart; anoint with 1–2 drops of black pepper, carrot seed or sage oil. (*Can promote confrontation.*)

• **GREEN TOURMALINE** eases the heart; frees rigid expectations.

• **OPAL** uncovers emotions; boosts male solar energy as well as female lunar energy.

• **RUBY** heals emotional wounds by soothing and strengthening heart energy; coaxes you to let go of heaviness, pain and negative emotions.

Incense
• **MEADOWSWEET** enhances love and calms your mind.

• **NAG CHAMPA** elevates your mood and develops your spiritual qualities.

• **ORRIS ROOT** lifts the veils of your emotions.

Heart-energy foods
Alongside green tea, green leafy vegetables and rosy apples, try:

• **LEAFY HERBS:** basil, coriander, marjoram, oregano, parsley.

• **LOTUS SEEDS (OR NUTS):** open your heart and enhance devotion.

YOGA ASANAS FOR ANAHATA ENERGY

The yoga poses shown here help to open your heart chakra. Include them in your regular practice, or use them before sitting for meditation. Some backbends not shown, such as *Salabhasana* (Locust Pose) and *Urdhva Dhanurasana* (Full Wheel Pose) have heart energy benefits, too, as do hugging, prayer, yoga breathing and acts of selfless service.

Dhanurasana: Bow Pose (a)

1 *Lie on your abdomen, bend your knees and take hold of your ankles.*
2 *Inhaling, lift your head, chest and legs away from the ground. Keep your elbows straight and aim to lift your legs as high as possible.*
3 *Look up and hold for 30 seconds. Then relax. Repeat 2–3 times.*

Ustrasana: Camel Pose (b)

1 *Sit on your heels. Reaching back slowly, catch hold of your heels.*
2 *Lift your hips as high as possible and bring them forward. Feel your heart chakra arching toward the sky. Gently drop your head back.*
3 *Hold the position for 10–30 seconds before releasing.*

Hanumanasana: Hanuman Pose (c)

1 *If you are flexible, slide one leg forward and the other back until you are supported by the ground. Place a cushion beneath your groin if necessary. As an easy alternative, kneel, then step your left foot forward, foot flat on the floor, heel directly beneath your knee.*
2 *Bring your palms together at your heart chakra. Visualize the Hindu monkey god Hanuman opening his chest to reveal God in his heart. Hold for 30–60 seconds, then repeat on the other side.*

(a)

(b)

(c)

Minor Chakras:
ACTIVATING YOUR HANDS

If you trip and hurt yourself, you often rub the painful area without thinking. This instinctive action activates the lesser-known chakra located on the palms of both hands, stimulating a flow of healing energy from your heart chakra. Although usually considered to be a minor chakra, the hand chakra is energetically important. It is an essential antenna, and without it we would have difficulty in receiving energetic information from the world and in transmitting energy outward.

When you stimulate or activate your hand chakra it becomes sensitized, and you become more aware of your energy fields. You may eventually go on to develop the ability to give energetic healing. The meditation below begins that sensitization process.

Hand Chakra Meditation

1 *Sit or stand and extend your arms in front of you. Keep them parallel to the ground and straighten your elbows. Rotate your right arm so that the right palm faces up and the left palm down (see below left).*
2 *Make fists and quickly release them, opening and closing your hands 20–30 times (see below right).*

3 Reverse the direction of your hands so that the palm that was facing upward is now facing downward, and vice versa. Repeat the rapid opening and closing fist movement.

4 Then turn your palms to face each other, keeping your hands open or "cupped" (see right). Slowly bring your palms toward each other. When your hands are about 10cm (4in) apart, see if you can feel a ball of energy between them. (Do not confuse this with body heat; it is more like a magnetic field floating between the palms.)

5 Move your palms away from each other and back again. Play with the energy, bouncing it from hand to hand.

6 Finally, hold one palm in front of your heart chakra, 10–12.5cm (4–5in) away from your body. Close your eyes, and move this hand in a circular direction, clockwise. After a few minutes, reverse the direction.

7 Move your hand 2.5–5cm (1–2in) closer to your chest and repeat the clockwise movements. Then swap hands. Try to experience the direct connection between the energy centre in your hands and your heart chakra before finishing the meditation.

VARIATIONS ON THE PRACTICE

To open and activate the chakra in the palm of each hand further, mix 1 drop of essential oil of rose and/or lavender according to preference in 1 tsp sweet almond oil and massage into your palms (first check the cautions on page 4). Rose links your hands to your heart and helps you to channel love energy. Lavender increases your sensitivity to another person's energetic vibrations. You might explore other activities that sensitize the hand chakra, such as clapping, kung fu, Reiki, Therapeutic Touch or the laying on of hands.

chapter 5

VISHUDDHA CHAKRA
YOUR COMMUNICATION CENTRE

The vishuddha, or throat, chakra is the bridge between your heart and your mind. A creative impulse may come to mind, but it can only begin to manifest in the world when you express it as speech, using vishuddha energy. If this bridge of communication is blocked, impulses are "choked", and ideas, hopes and dreams, unable to travel down the chakra system ("be taken to heart"), remain unrealized.

The literal translation of the Sanskrit word vishuddha is "the pure place": this chakra presides over your will, your power of choice and your sense of truth. It is here that you take responsibility for decisions and speak up for what you believe in. This is also where you develop a spiritual voice. This chapter's meditations show the importance of expressing the truth in your heart and the ideas in your mind.

Understanding
YOUR VISHUDDHA CHAKRA

As we move up through the chakras, we reach the last one to have a physical element associated with it – the throat chakra. The element of this chakra is *akasha*, a Sanskrit term that translates as "ether", "limitless space" or "sky" (it is symbolized by the colour blue). This element is matter in its purest, most subtle form and it pervades not just this chakra, but all the chakras we have looked at so far. Thus, the anahata chakra contains ether as well as air; the manipura chakra possesses ether and air in addition to fire; the swadhisthana chakra contains fire, air and ether as well as water; and the earth of the muladhara chakra comprises water, fire, air and ether. Only ether (in the vishuddha chakra) is pure, and looks up the chakra system to "touch" pure consciousness.

The sense associated with your throat chakra is hearing (ether being the medium of sound and vibration). And unblocking your throat chakra involves not only listening more to others and developing empathy, but also tuning into your own heart and spending time in silence. Working with your vishuddha chakra helps you to recognize that silence can be golden and full of meaning. Yet, it also allows you to recognize that commands, such as "be quiet" can block the throat chakra.

When your vishuddha chakra is open and well-balanced, you are able to express your beliefs, creativity and emotional needs openly, without fearing others' opinions. But a blockage in the throat chakra often distorts your ability to communicate: you might speak half-truths or untruths, even if unknowingly; and you might put on a brave face rather than attempt to express inner turmoil or dissatisfaction. This not only hampers communication, but also stifles your ability to

---

Chakra meaning: *the pure place* **Element:** *ether (space)*
Sound vibration: HAM **Sense association:** *hearing*

stand up for what you believe in and to bring your dreams to fruition. Alternatively, you might suffer from verbal diarrhoea that drains your vishuddha energy. Many negative habits are linked to imbalances in the throat chakra – for example, gossiping, over-eating, smoking and alcoholism. Obsessive behaviour may also stem from an inability to assimilate energy and communicate in healthy ways.

In your physical body, the throat chakra governs the organs used in communication and artistic endeavour – your mouth, tongue, throat, ears, eyes and hands. Energetic imbalances often play a role in speech complaints, eating disorders, symptoms of stress and even in deafness.

Stimulating your throat chakra brings the gifts of a melodious voice, an impressive command of speech and the ability to compose poetry, to interpret the written word, to understand messages within dreams and to be a good teacher, especially on a spiritual level. The vishuddha chakra is ruled by the planet Jupiter, which represents the teacher in the Indian tradition. Intensive meditation on the vishuddha chakra increases your ability to understand the essence of the world's great scriptures. Meditating on this chakra brings insights into the past, present and future – and the ability to communicate that wisdom.

WORKING WITH VISHUDDHA ENERGY

As you follow the meditations in this chapter, ask yourself the following questions. They can help you to see how you block your vishuddha energy and to understand how you might rebalance it.

- *Do I often fail to keep promises? How can I improve this?*
- *Do I ever use my words to hurt others? Or do I use them to try to empower others?*
- *Am I expressing myself honestly? If not, how can I start doing this?*
- *Am I prone to gossiping? If so, why do I do this?*

Meditating on a Yantra:
TUNING INTO YOUR THROAT CHAKRA

As you study the chakra's image or *yantra*, think back to the root chakra's black elephant (see page 39), a symbol of the solid physical world. Sense how this chakra's white elephant signifies ether, which dissolves, purifies and unifies the gross elements of the lower chakras and material world.

Yantra Meditation

1 *Cover a low table with a clean cloth, then prop up the chakra illustration opposite on top, so that it is slightly below eye level when you are seated. Light a candle and some incense (see page 119).*

2 *Sit comfortably upright, preferably cross-legged with your back straight (see page 16). Take 10–20 deep breaths, then let your breathing settle.*

3 *With half-closed eyes, gaze at the 16 smoky-purple petals that form the border. In Indian symbology, 16 is sacred to the Divine Mother, and at the throat chakra, she is known as Vak or Vani Devi, the personification of speech. Each petal contains one of the vowels in the Sanskrit alphabet. The word* vishuddha *means "pure", and vowels are thought to be the purest sounds.*

4 *Move your gaze inward, to the downward-pointing triangle. It symbolizes lower chakra energy funnelled up through the throat to the higher centres.*

5 *Look further inward at the circle that represents ether, the element of the throat chakra. This stands for the sacred void that lies beyond the elements. Sense its rarified purity. Airavata, the white elephant of Indian myth appears in the circle. He reaches down with his seven trunks to raise the elements of the physical world into the clouds, connecting earth with heaven.*

6 *Finally, let your gaze rise from the blue circle to the Sanskrit character. It reads* HAM, *the mantra of ether. Repeat it silently, thinking of Hamsa, the white swan that symbolizes the divine spirit or liberated self. After meditating for 20 minutes or more, open your eyes. Practise daily.*

Progressing further

When the yantra is so familiar that you can visualize it without looking at it, sit with your spine straight, close your eyes and focus on your throat. Visualize the yantra as an energy pattern here, its rays and mantra HAM radiating outward. Meditate on this for at least 30 minutes.

Meditating on the Elements:
THE ETHER ELEMENT

Meditating on the vishuddha chakra's element ether, in the form of sky, is said to enhance mental strength and the ability to absorb yourself in deep meditation. It also reveals knowledge beyond written words and heightens your capacity to explain and clarify. You will gradually become aware that there is limitless space within your being, just as the sky extends infinitely beyond the earth's atmosphere. Allow yourself to be open to the unlimited possibilities that this presents.

The meditation opposite is useful when you feel restricted or hemmed in. It is best performed outside on a clear day with a good view of the sky, although you can sit inside, looking out of a window.

"The quintessence of ether is to visualize it as a sky that is as clear and bright as the pure waters of the ocean. HAM is its mantra. By fixing the mind on this element for two hours one opens the gates of liberation."
GHERANDA SAMHITA, 3.80–81

Ether Meditation

---

1 Sit comfortably in a meditative position, preferably cross-legged. Make sure that your back is straight.

2 Gaze at the sky, aware that it represents the element ether and has the quality of limitless space. Although the sky is actually colourless, note how its blue appearance corresponds to that of the throat chakra.

3 Next, start witnessing your breath. Exhale tension and inhale strength. Be aware of the parts of your body that are in contact with the ground. Direct your breath into those areas and observe what happens. Feel yourself expanding downward. You may experience a heaviness, or a lightness so extreme that you feel you are floating.

4 Now bring your attention to the left side of your body and feel your energy radiating toward this side. Send your breath to your left leg, arm, neck, cheek and temple. Feel yourself expanding to the left.

5 Next, turn your attention to the whole right side of your body, and feel your energy radiating here. Direct your breath in the same way as before and feel yourself expanding to the right.

6 Now be aware of the back of your body. Feel energy radiating from the bottom to the top: from your buttocks, up through your back and arms to the nape of your neck and the back of your head. Send breath into these parts and experience a sense of expanding backward.

7 Next feel the front of your body. Notice how far the energy radiates into your legs, belly, chest, arms, throat and face. Send your breath into these parts. Feel yourself expanding toward the front.

8 Now observe your upper body parts and how energy radiates toward them. Breathe into your shoulders and head. Sense upward expansion.

9 Finally, feel yourself expanding in all directions simultaneously, fully aware that you are pervaded by ether. Repeat the affirmation, "I am at one with the universe" until you feel that nothing limits your nature.

Mouna:
OBSERVING SILENCE

Excessive talking tends to distract the mind and make it very difficult to focus inward and meditate. Try subduing your speech and learning to listen more. You will probably find that, after some time, you can control your senses and your mind more easily and that all forms of communication seem more meaningful. By creating silence within your mind, you begin to become aware of what others are really saying – not only with their voices, but also with their facial expressions and their bodies.

Deep listening is a skill that creates a profound connection with other people at the throat chakra and often leads to more compassionate connections at your heart chakra. The practice of keeping silence, which in Sanskrit is known as *mouna*, is a powerful exercise that can help you to conserve, purify and strengthen the energy of your throat chakra. As you practise the Mouna Meditation opposite, you will begin, through a process of self-analysis, to make sure that your words coincide with your actions – and to ensure that both your words and your actions remain in tune with your thoughts.

"One should speak the truth and speak it pleasantly; one should not speak the truth in an unpleasant manner nor should one speak untruth because it is pleasing; this is the eternal law."
LAWS OF MANU

Mouna Meditation

1 *To observe silence you need to choose a time or a day when you do not need to work or mix with other people. While you are keeping silent, you can practise yoga asanas or pranayama breathing exercises, or do some simple manual work. But do not listen to music, watch television, perform any type of fast exercise or do anything that requires intellectual focus, such as reading.*

2 *As you decrease the external "noise" around you, note the busyness of your internal mental environment. In the early days of practising Mouna Meditation, notice the great number of thoughts that arise to try to get you to break your silence: you might suddenly remember a phone call you have to make, or old worries, problems and emotions might surface. Do not allow yourself to become involved with these concerns. Just watch the thoughts as though they are bubbles, which will soon "pop" or float away. Your anxieties will no longer exist, and it will become easier to remain silent both internally and externally.*

3 *Try to introduce the increased mental awareness that this practice brings into your everyday life. Before speaking, "edit" your words. Say only what is required and what is truthful. As your silent practice stills your bubbling thoughts and surging emotions, notice how words begin to have greater power, when you do utter them.*

4 *Over time, build up your Mouna Meditation practice until you can observe external silence for at least one hour daily. Or, if possible, spend one day a week in total silence. It is recommended that you eat a meal in complete silence at least once each week.*

Brahmari:
BUMBLE-BEE BREATHING

Brahmari is a vocal meditation that resembles the buzzing of a bee and helps to open and balance your throat chakra. It is highly recommended as a practice if you are a singer, teacher or someone who has to speak in public – or if you simply would like to improve your speech and communication skills.

Deep joy and contentment are often experienced through doing the Brahmari Meditation opposite. It brings a sense of great inner peace as your mind becomes free from chatter. The exercise improves your concentration, memory and confidence, and helps to banish feelings of self-doubt as well as the urge to gossip. Because Brahmari stimulates and purifies your energetic centre of communication, you will probably find that it helps you to develop the ability to listen intently and to communicate on a more profound level. You may discover your true inner voice and learn how to measure your words.

If you practise Brahmari on a regular basis, you are likely to notice how sweet and melodious your voice becomes. With regular practice, the meditation can also help to alleviate many throat problems, such as hoarseness and a weak voice. The extended exhalation used in the meditation (see steps 5–6) is especially beneficial for pregnant women, as it is an excellent preparation for breathing during labour.

When you first practise, don't worry if you feel a slight increase in body heat: this is simply your blood circulation quickening.

"Fill in the air rapidly, making the sound of a male bee, practise retention and again exhale it, making the sound of a female bee humming. The great yogis by a constant practice of this feel an indescribable joy in in their hearts. This is Brahmari."
HATHA YOGA PRADIPIKA, 2.68

Brahmari Meditation

1 *Kneel with your buttocks on your heels, or sit on a chair so that your abdomen and chest are unobstructed. Rest your palms on your knees.*

2 *With your mouth and lips gently closed, tighten the glottis at the back of your throat. Keep your head erect and relax your neck muscles.*

3 *Inhale strongly through both nostrils, vibrating the soft palate and making a snoring sound. Feel the snoring inhalation energize your throat. Some people describe this as the sound you make when you are trying to clear your throat. Yoga scriptures liken the sensation to the buzzing of a large black bumble-bee.*

4 *Hold your breath for a few moments — for as long as feels comfortable. During this slight retention, let your mind experience the element associated with the throat chakra: ether, or space.*

5 *When you are ready, exhale through both nostrils, making a high-pitched humming sound, like the buzzing of a small honey bee. Aim to exhale all the air in your lungs.*

6 *Repeat the exercise 5—10 times. Be aware of the sensation of the vibration in your throat, mouth, cheeks and lips. Notice how the humming helps you to regulate your breathing and to achieve a longer and more complete exhalation.*

7 *When you have finished, close your eyes and sit quietly for 20—30 minutes, breathing normally and focusing your attention on your throat chakra. Retain awareness of the feeling and the reverberation of the humming sound as you go about your daily activities.*

The Soundless Sound
MEDITATING ON *OM*

OM, or *AUM*, is the sound of the infinite – the most abstract and highest mantra, within which all other mantras are said to be contained. *OM* is the manifested symbol of the original vibration, the transcendental soundless sound reputed by Hindu texts to have caused the universe to come into being. We might compare the concept to the scientific theory of the "big bang". Although *OM* is the mantra of the ajna, or third-eye, chakra, its vibration manifests in the physical world through the vishuddha chakra when it is chanted out loud.

Chanting *OM* is recommended to release blockages that might be present in your throat region and to make your voice more resonant. The sound is believed to have a positive effect on the nervous system, to strengthen the respiratory system and to energize every part of the body. Chanting its three syllables (*A-U-M*) sets up rebalancing vibrations in your body while awakening latent psychic and mental powers.

Because of its universality, *OM* is a useful and powerful mantra that anyone can use. You can chant it whether you are on your own or with a group of people. Some spiritual teachers like to open meetings or classes by chanting *OM* with the group; it is thought to enhance communication. When sessions close with a resonant *OM*, the chant is reputed to equip participants with a deeper understanding of the subject studied.

"AUM stands for the supreme Reality.
It is a symbol for what was, what is and what shall be.
AUM also represents what lies beyond past, present and future."
MANDUKYA UPANISHAD, VERSE 1

OM Chanting

1 *Sit in a comfortable upright meditation position. If you are working in a group, it is best to sit facing each other or in a circle.*

2 *Close your eyes and take a deep breath in. Open your mouth wide and begin to loudly chant the initial syllable,* AAAH, *keeping your mouth wide open. Let the sound begin in the pit of your abdomen.*

3 *Gradually round your lips to allow the sound to morph into* OU. *Feel it move up through your chest and throat region.*

4 *Continue rounding your lips more tightly to form the final sound,* MMMMM. *Let the sound vibrate in your head and face, especially in your sinus cavities.*

5 *Take a deep breath and slowly repeat the* OM *sound, making each part of the sound as long as possible. Try not to let your mind drift: keep focused on the chanting and the vibration, tuning it with your breath. Feel the mantra vibrating in your throat chakra.*

6 *Continue chanting this elongated* OM *for at least 20 minutes. Make the sound gradually softer and softer, until you are whispering and then just humming it. Then make the sound gradually louder again.*

THE COMPONENTS OF *OM*

Though usually written *OM*, the mantra consists of three parts:

PART OF MANTRA	AAAH	OU	MMMMM
SOUND MADE WITH:	Mouth wide open	Mouth rounded	Lips shut
SOUND VIBRATES IN:	Abdomen	Chest	Head and sinuses
REPRESENTS:	Past	Present	Future
STATE OF CONSCIOUSNESS:	Waking state	Dream state	Deep sleep
RELATED TO:	Physical body	Mental / subtle body	Beyond the mind

Tools for Working with
VISHUDDHA ENERGY

Use the tools suggested here to support your meditation, helping you toward free-flowing energy at your throat chakra. This brings freedom from non-physical thirst and hunger (such as thirst for knowledge and hunger for love). If you are pregnant or have a medical condition, consult a medical practitioner before using essential oils or herbs.

Flower essences

To work intensively with vishuddha energy, use these essences before meditation. Place 4 drops under your tongue (or take in water).

• BLUEBELL simplifies issues; connects you with your surroundings.

• BORAGE helps you to express and transform sorrow and depression.

• LARCH opens the vishuddha chakra; releases "failure"; unlocks creativity.

• LOBELIA helps you to speak up for what you believe in.

• SNAPDRAGON balances energy between the sacral and throat chakras for harmonious verbal expression; frees creative energy.

• BLACKBERRY encourages you to speak joyfully about what you believe to be true in a way that will be heard and is helpful to others.

Essential oils

Use in a pre-meditation bath: blend 3–5 drops of essential oil into 1 tsp jojoba, sweet almond or olive carrier oil; pour into running water as you fill the bath.

• BERGAMOT helps you to calmly express truths that arise as your heart chakra opens. (*Use FCF grade.*)

• CHAMOMILE allows you to voice truth without anger or resentment.

• EUCALYPTUS helps if you feel "frozen"; aids spontaneous expression.

• SANDALWOOD motivates your creative energies at your throat chakra, helping you to come up with fresh solutions; encourages wider vision.

•TEA TREE shifts vishuddha energy; helps you to reach your potential.

• PEPPERMINT stimulates you to lead a more ethical life.

Crystals, gems and stones

Wear in jewelry, place near the chakra or simply hold before meditation. Gemstones are especially supportive for this chakra when set in silver, which enhances speech and strengthens your faith in your higher self.

•TURQUOISE improves speech, communication and healing.

• AMBER works best when it is touching the skin; gives you a "golden tongue" – wear it at your throat for clear and confident speech.

• AQUAMARINE enhances communication; activates and cleanses your throat chakra; useful for couples working out differences.

• AMAZONITE opens your throat, heart and solar-plexus chakras for greater self-expression, artistic creativity and healing.

•LAPIS LAZULI energizes; enhances creativity; purifies thoughts; lets you tap into your inner power and higher self; the gold-flecked dark blue form enhances truthfulness, openness, intuition and psychic ability.

•AMETHYST aids recovery from addiction; eases compulsive behaviour.

Incense

• MYRRH RESIN deepens prayer and meditation; especially useful when you feel "stuck". Place on charcoal to burn.

Empowering foods

Easily digested chakra-stimulating foods that bring sweetness to life include:

• NATURAL SWEETENERS: fruits and their juices; honey and propolis.

• PURIFYING HERBS: horehound and slippery elm, either lozenges or tea.

YOGA ASANAS FOR VISHUDDHA ENERGY

Include the following poses in your regular yoga practice or use them before meditation to stimulate your throat chakra. Other practices that work with your throat chakra include singing, debating and simply gargling daily with salt water.

UJJAYI BREATH

Ujjayi breathing stimulates, unblocks and strengthens the throat chakra. Sit with your legs crossed and back straight. Open your mouth and breathe out HAAA. Close your mouth; when you inhale, make the same HAAA sound through your nose. Exhale through your nose and repeat HAAA. Repeat several times.

Sarvangasana: Shoulderstand

1 *Lie on your back, legs together. Lift them to the sky. Supporting your back with your hands, roll onto your shoulders, elbows pointing away. If your neck is tense, roll down and try with a folded blanket under your shoulders.*
2 *Move your hands onto your upper back, fingers pointing toward your spine. Straighten your back as far as possible. Extend your legs, relaxing your calves and feet. Keep all your weight on your elbows, rather than your neck. Build up to 3 minutes in the pose.*
3 *Slowly roll your back down, taking your arms to the floor. Then gently lower your legs, keeping your head on the ground.*

Halasana: Plough Pose

1 *Once you are in Shoulderstand (see left), if you feel comfortable, lower your feet to the floor behind your head. If your feet touch the ground easily, lengthen your arms, keeping them flat on the floor.*
2 *Try to remain in this pose for at least 1 minute. Slowly roll out of the pose, keeping your arms and head on the ground.*

Simhasana: Lion Pose

1 *Kneel and bend forward to place your hands on your knees or thighs. Inhale deeply through your nose.*
2 *Exhale fully through your mouth. As you do so, open your mouth wide, stick out your tongue, widen your eyes and roar like a lion. Repeat 2–3 times before relaxing.*

Minor Chakras:

YOUR TORTOISE CHAKRA

Below your throat chakra and above your heart chakra lies a minor chakra with a radiant energy pattern that resembles a tortoise, or *kurma* in Sanskrit. Meditation on this energy centre brings about a calmness that is sometimes likened to the peace of hibernation.

The tortoise is a universal symbol of stability and steady resolve. Once he has decided to pull in his head and legs, nothing and no one can change his mind. In Indian mythology, it is a tortoise that supports the universe. The four legs, head and tail of the tortoise may be seen as an analogy for the five senses plus the mind. The ability of the tortoise to draw in his extremities and remain peaceful within himself is symbolic of the yoga practice of *pratyahara*. Though usually translated as "withdrawal of the senses", this practice is better described as withdrawing mental energy from the senses.

The senses are like electrical appliances that only function when plugged into an energy source. For example, if you are absorbed in a book, you might not hear the telephone ring: there is nothing wrong with your ears, but your mental energy is being channelled to your eyes. In pratyahara you deliberately "unplug" your senses from their energy source. When you sit to begin meditation, try to close down your senses. Do not allow energy to travel from your mind to your eyes, nose, ears, skin or mouth; nor to your hands or feet (the Sanskrit word for senses encompasses the organs of action). This means that you stop seeing, smelling, hearing, touching, tasting, speaking, moving or working. When mental energy no longer escapes, you are practising pratyahara and take on the qualities of the steady, peaceful tortoise.

"By steady focus on the tortoise at the pit of the throat, calmness of body and mind is acquired."
PATANJALI, *RAJA YOGA SUTRAS*, 3.31

Tortoise Chakra Meditation

1 *Sit in a comfortable meditation position, preferably with your legs crossed and your back straight. Take a few minutes to allow your breathing to settle into a natural rhythm.*

2 *Close your eyes and take your awareness inside your body. Become conscious of the location of your tortoise chakra in the region of your upper sternum (breastbone), just above the point at which your trachea, or windpipe, branches out to form your bronchial tubes (see annotated photograph, page 15).*

3 *As you direct your awareness to the site of your tortoise chakra, consciously allow your breathing to slow down. Then mentally watch your breath as it passes through your tortoise energy centre. Do nothing but maintain this focus. It "unplugs" your senses and is more effective than instructing them to stop being active.*

4 *Every time your mind starts to drift during the meditation, simply direct your focus back to your breath at your tortoise chakra.*

5 *Try to continue this meditation for at least 20 minutes a day, gradually building up to 45 minutes. With practice, you will begin to experience the calm inner peace and profound emotional stability that comes about when your senses are stilled and your tortoise chakra is open and in balance.*

chapter 6

AJNA CHAKRA

THE SEAT OF YOUR WISDOM

Often referred to as the third eye or mind's eye, the ajna, or brow, chakra is the command centre for your subtle body. It manages not only your five senses, but also your conscious and subconscious mind, at the same time as regulating the other chakras and their related energy channels.

Located just above and between your eyebrows, the brow chakra forms the final junction of the three major nadi energy channels. The ida (left channel) and pingala (right channel) terminate here, while the central sushumna continues to the crown chakra and higher levels of consciousness.

Another name for this chakra is jnana-padma, "knowledge-bestowing lotus". The meditations in this chapter bestow wisdom, clarity of vision and increased intuition, allowing you to begin to see life's bigger picture.

Understanding

YOUR AJNA CHAKRA

The ajna chakra presides over your mind and your sense of self. Although this chakra strictly speaking has no element associated with it, the mind could be thought of as the brow chakra's element, since the mind controls the senses and vital energy. Of all the chakras, the energy here has the most powerful effect on your personality. This chakra is the seat of your judgment, your emotional intelligence and your notion of reality, rationality and wisdom. Six spiritual "powers" are associated with this chakra: unobstructed meditation, perfect concentration, the ability to direct your undivided attention, thought-control, *samadhi* or the super-conscious state, and the attainment of enlightenment.

When your ajna chakra is open and balanced, you witness the world without judgment and you perceive everything that is within the scope of the senses, as well as all that is beyond them (this centre is the source of intuition and psychic perception). Separately, the ida and pingala channels are bound in the present; yet here, where their energies merge, you enter the timeless realm and can learn from the past, recognize current trends and also "see" and plan for the future.

WORKING WITH AJNA ENERGY

As you follow the meditations in this chapter, ask yourself the following questions. They can help you to see how you block your ajna energy and to understand how you might rebalance it.

• *Am I generally able to see the bigger picture? How might I see it better?*

• *Can I hear my ego speaking? Are my heart and mind in agreement?*

• *Do I set my standards too high? If not, could I achieve more with concerted effort?*

• *How could life be better? How can I work toward this?*

If the flow of energy at your ajna chakra is healthy, your mind is focused and you are blessed with a vivid, yet disciplined imagination. You are likely to be charismatic, highly intuitive, unattached to material possessions and possibly prone to experiencing psychic phenomena.

If your ajna energy is deficient, you might lack discipline and inner vision, have a poor memory, fear success, communicate poorly and/or fail to understand subtle signals, resulting in an inclination to set your sights and standards too low. If, on the other hand, the energy of your ajna chakra is overbearing, you might be unable to tune into, or trust, your intuition. To compensate, some people can become dogmatic, self-righteous, authoritarian and arrogant, or overly intellectual and excessively rational. They display over-abundant "head" energy, but are totally lacking in "heart", because they have depleted the energy reserves of their lower chakras by drawing energy too far upward. This is damaging as the ajna chakra requires the support of stable lower chakras. Fortunately, a healthy ajna chakra encourages balance in the lower chakras. In fact, for this reason, many yogis begin chakra work at the brow centre – it is also the easiest chakra to rouse, often helps the other chakras to open, and, once open, counteracts negative consequences of imbalance in other chakras.

In your physical body, the ajna chakra governs your eyes, ears, nose and the base of your skull. An energetic imbalance may often be a factor in vision problems, headaches, migraines and dizziness, and can also play a part in confusion, poor memory, insomnia and acute sinusitis.

By working with ajna energy, you enhance your intuition and gain a clearer view of your purpose in life. You are likely to become more creative, developing the ability to think symbolically and to find ever-new ways of looking at the world. In doing so, you break through the *Rudra Granthi*, the energetic knot of ego-awareness and intellectual pride (see page 33), and move nearer the ultimate goal: cosmic awareness.

Meditating on a Yantra:

TUNING INTO YOUR BROW CHAKRA

Visualizing the ajna chakra's image or *yantra* (see right), allows you to sense how the main currents within your energetic body come together here. As you do so, you begin to integrate their complementary energies within your body and mind, a fusion which is symbolized by Ardhanarishwara, the Indian deity who presides over this chakra. This half male and half female figure represents the coming together of the opposing qualities of the major nadis (see chart, page 29).

Yantra Meditation

1 *Cover a low table with a clean cloth, then prop up the chakra illustration opposite on top, slightly below eye level when you are seated in front of it. Light a candle and some incense (see page 135).*

2 *Sit comfortably upright, preferably cross-legged with your back straight (see page 16). Take 10–20 deep breaths; let your breath settle.*

3 *Start by getting a general impression of the picture. Most of the chakra symbols resemble a lotus flower, but this one is different. See how its diagram of radiant energy contains a luminous white circle with a pure white petal on either side. Think about how each petal stands for the opposing yet complementary energies of Siva (masculine, passive energy) and Shakti (feminine, active energy) in your body, represented here by the male-female figure. Consider how the two main nadis, ida and pingala, join at your brow chakra (see pages 28–29).*

4 *Bring your focus to the central circle. The Sanskrit letter there represents* OM, *the mantra of the brow chakra. This sacred monosyllable symbolizes absolute consciousness.*

5 *If desired, you can now follow the* OM *Chanting meditation on pages 116–17. Practise the Yantra Meditation for at least 20 minutes daily.*

Progressing further

After some months practising this Yantra Meditation, observe how your focus becomes so intense that you begin to develop enhanced intuition and deeper empathy with others. At that point, instead of meditating with the image, sit, close your eyes, bring your focus to your brow centre and visualize the picture between your eyebrows for at least 30 minutes.

Finding Inner Silence:
STILLING YOUR MIND

Your mind controls your senses and the prana in your body. However, if your mind is restless, you will be overcome by wave after wave of thought, sensation and desire: a constant undercurrent of possibilities is likely to tug at your consciousness, resulting in very little inner peace.

A lake or an ocean is often used as an analogy for the mind in yogic philosophy. When they are calm, there is nothing to churn up the mud or sand at the bottom and there are no waves to disturb the clarity of the water. Similarly, when your thoughts subside in the lake or ocean of your mind, you feel peace and experience lucidity. The Mind-lake Visualization opposite helps you to experience such stillness.

"When the thought waves are stilled, the see-er experiences his own true splendour."
PATANJALI, *YOGA SUTRAS*, I.3

Mind-lake Visualization

1 Sit in a comfortable meditative position, preferably with your legs crossed and back straight. Close your eyes. Take a few deep breaths, then allow your breath to settle into a slow, natural rhythm.

2 Bring your awareness to your brow centre and picture your mind as a lake. At first, you may see many waves on the surface of your mind-lake. These are your thoughts and current concerns.

3 Now imagine that someone has dropped a large, beautiful diamond into the water. Gently try to see this gemstone shining brightly on the lakebed. If you strive hard or actively think, you will stir up the waters, which will become muddy and you will be unable to see the diamond. Whenever thoughts interrupt, do not drive them away – this will only encourage them to return, increased in strength. Instead, try to gently focus all your attention on trying to see the diamond.

4 Slow down the flow of your breath and allow it to become smooth. Your mind, which is closely connected to your breath, will respond by becoming calmer and any ripples will gradually subside, so that, at last, you can see the diamond clearly.

5 Holding on to the image of the diamond, notice how stilling your mind and focusing on the gem brings a silent, profound inner calm. Let the image of the diamond fade and allow the silence to envelop you by focusing all your senses on it. Imagine that you can see, smell and touch this silence. It is the peace "which passeth all understanding", spoken of in the Bible and other spiritual writings.

6 Continue meditating in this way for at least 20 minutes. Then, stretch your legs and sit quietly for a few minutes, dwelling in the sensation of inner peace. Try to retain this awareness as you return to daily life. As your practice develops, build up this meditation to 45 minutes.

Tratak:
CANDLE GAZING

Tratak, or "steady gazing", is an excellent form of meditation for purifying and strengthening the ajna chakra. It is most commonly practised, as in the exercise opposite, by gazing at the flame of a candle for some time without blinking. However, you can also practise tratak by using a visual image that stands out strongly against its background as a point of focus, such as a black dot on a white wall, or you can fix your gaze on the tip of your nose or turn your eyes upward to the space between your eyebrows (see page 139).

Mentally, the exercise promotes intense concentration. Physical advantages of gazing at one point include a strengthening of the eye muscles and of the nerve centres in the forehead. And when you inhibit the blink reflex, your eyes shed tears, which is cleansing for the eyes, tear ducts and sinuses.

Before you begin the Tratak Meditation opposite, place a candle at an arm's distance away, perhaps on a chair or a low table in front of you. The candle should be at eye-level when you are sitting. Light the candle, then turn off any electric lights or draw the curtains to darken the room. Make sure that there are no draughts in the room before you start your meditation: the flame must remain steady, not flicker.

"Look (without blinking the eyelids) at a minute object with your mind concentrated until tears come into the eyes. This is called trataka *by the gurus. By* trataka, *all diseases of the eye and sloth are removed. So it should be carefully preserved secretly as a golden casket."*
HATHAYOGA PRADIPIKA, 2–31, 32

Tratak Meditation

1 *Sit in a comfortable meditation position, preferably with your legs crossed, facing the candle. Make sure that your spine and head are extending upward and that your body is relaxed. Join your hands together loosely and rest them in your lap.*

2 *Open your eyes wide and look with a steady gaze at the flame, trying not to blink. Check your face and eye muscles for tension and consciously relax it. Do not allow your eyes to cross or to lose focus (you will know this has happened if you start to see multiple images). Look deeply into the flame. Notice that it has several rings of differing colours. Hold your gaze on them for about 1 minute.*

3 *Then gently close your eyes. Relax your eye muscles and visualize the flame you have been looking at. See it with your mind's eye. Do not concentrate on the "physical" image of a flame that lingers after the optic nerve has been stimulated by bright light. Instead, use your mind to draw a mental picture of the flame, including its rings of light in various colours. Hold the mental image of the candle firmly at the point between your eyebrows for 1 minute to strengthen the chakra.*

4 *Repeat steps 2 and 3, this time keeping your eyes open for 3 minutes in step 2. Then, when you close your eyes in step 3, sit for 10–20 minutes, keeping the candle image firmly fixed in your mind's eye. As you become more practised at the meditation, gradually increase the time you gaze at the candle in step 2, to 5 or even 10 minutes.*

Tools for Working with
AJNA ENERGY

The following tools support you in enhancing your concentration and clearing stagnant energy at the brow chakra. Bathing or washing your hands and face before meditation can also help to cleanse yourself of other energies. If you are pregnant or have a medical condition, consult a medical practitioner before fasting or using essential oils.

Indian anointing powders

Traditionally, three powders are applied to the third eye to enhance meditation. You can buy them from holistic stores or online.

• *VIBHUTI*, holy ash, represents the destructive aspect of the divine and rids you of negativity. After washing your face, draw three lines on your forehead (left to right) with your right little, ring and middle fingers.

• *CHANDANA*, cooling sandalwood paste, represents the balancing aspect of divine consciousness. After applying *vibhuti*, add a dot of this paste with your right ring finger to balance energy flow at your ajna chakra.

• *KUMKUM*, powdered flowers, represents the creative aspect of the universe. After applying *vibhuti* and *chandana*, add a dot of *kumkum* with your right ring finger to stimulate and open your brow centre.

Flower essences

Place 4 drops under the tongue (or take in water) before meditating.

• CLEMATIS focuses awareness; awakens your evaluation of the present.

• CLARY SAGE clears intuition-blocking congestion; directs your vision.

• PETUNIA develops wonder; encourages you to reach for your dreams.

"Here the Seed of Immortality bursts forth, like an autumn moon. One who meditates on Ajna can extract the milk of Reality from the concoction that is the world phenomena."
SIVA SAMHITA, 5.97

Essential oils

For a pre-meditation bath, blend 3–5 drops oil into 1 tsp carrot seed oil and pour into running water as you fill the bath.

• LEMON refreshes and cleanses the energy of the ajna chakra.

• JUNIPER clarifies inner vision; purges the mind of self-doubt.

• ROSEMARY connects you with spiritual truths; protects you from negativity; clears your thoughts.

• SANDALWOOD has a cooling effect on the emotions; calms the mind; conteracts any tendency to over-analyze.

• LAVENDER harmonizes this chakra with the other chakras.

Crystals, gems and stones

Wear in jewelry, place near the chakra or simply hold the stone prior to meditation.

• AMETHYST draws energy to the higher realms; brings calm and clarity where there is anxiety or confusion; wear it to access intuition.

• CAT'S EYE OR TIGER'S EYE strengthens the connection between the crown and root chakras; anoint with 2 drops of frankincense oil.

• TURQUOISE enhances psychic connections; strengthens and aligns the nadis, the chakras and the body's energy fields; place on the brow.

Incense

• FRANKINCENSE RESIN deepens and slows the breath; sharpens the mind; brings you into a meditative state. Place on charcoal to burn.

• SANDALWOOD clears and focuses the mind.

Fasting

Abstaining from food frees the body and mind to focus on spiritual matters. If you find fasting on water for a day or so too difficult, drink only fruit juices or eat juicy fruits (but avoid starchy bananas).

YOGA ASANAS FOR AJNA ENERGY

As you gain in confidence, build up your practice of *Ardha Sirshasana* (Half Headstand), stage by stage. Pay particular attention to keeping your bodyweight safely on your elbows, not your head or neck. As ajna is the realm of the mind, positive "mind" games, such as crossword puzzles and sudoku, are valuable for strengthening ajna energy.

Ardha Sirshasana: Half Headstand

Stage 1

Sit on your heels and grasp each elbow with your opposite hand in front of you. Then place your arms on the ground in front of you, release your hands from your elbows and interlink your fingers to make a tripod shape between your elbows and hands.

Stage 2

Place your head on the ground with the back of your skull pressing against your clasped hands. Slowly straighten your knees, then walk your feet forward until your hips are directly aligned over your head. Only continue to stage 3 when you feel fully comfortable here.

Stage 3

Bend your knees without letting your hips drop, then lift your feet up toward your buttocks, keeping your knees bent. Do not jump or use fast movements: come into the pose slowly. Try to build up to 3 minutes in total in the pose, breathing deeply and keeping your focus at the point between your eyebrows. Come down slowly and rest with your head on the floor for a few minutes.

Minor Chakras:
YOUR SOMA CHAKRA

Just above the top of your palate lies a minor chakra known as the *soma* or *indu* chakra. This is the energetic centre linked with the serene energy of the moon, and meditation on this chakra helps you to release tension and anxiety, cool anger and experience a peaceful, contented sense of calm. By working with this chakra, you also gain the power to control the elements associated with the other chakras.

The soma chakra is stimulated by inhaling through your left nostril or by *Nasagra Drishti* (Nasal Gazing) – see opposite. It can be located by placing your awareness just inside the inner arch of your left eyebrow. Visualize it here as an ethereal, snow-white lotus containing 16 petals. This chakra is said to be the source of a "divine nectar" of immortality that

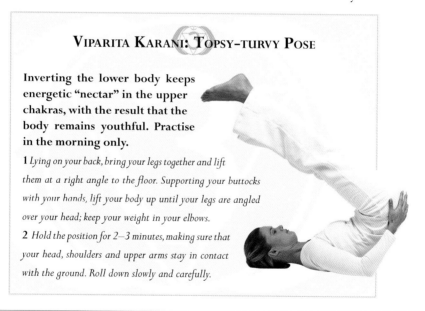

VIPARITA KARANI: TOPSY-TURVY POSE

Inverting the lower body keeps energetic "nectar" in the upper chakras, with the result that the body remains youthful. Practise in the morning only.

1 *Lying on your back, bring your legs together and lift them at a right angle to the floor. Supporting your buttocks with your hands, lift your body up until your legs are angled over your head; keep your weight in your elbows.*

2 *Hold the position for 2–3 minutes, making sure that your head, shoulders and upper arms stay in contact with the ground. Roll down slowly and carefully.*

"He who drinks the soma juice with a concentrated mind, doubtlessly conquers death."
HATHA YOGA PRADIPIKA, 3.44

has the power to wash away impurities. The energetic nectar is thought to seep out of the "cave", or hollow space, between the hemispheres of the brain. Most of the time, this youth-preserving nectar flows down through the soma chakra and the other energy centres beneath it until it reaches the solar plexus, where it is unfortunately "burnt off" by the fire of the manipura chakra. The result is that your youthful energy is constantly dissipated. One of the best ways to block this downward loss of energy is to practise the restorative yoga posture *Viparita Karani* (Topsy-turvy Pose; see box, left). Several ancient yogic scriptures claim that if you can stop the downward flow of divine nectar, you will remain forever young and filled with vitality and stamina. It is probably best to interpret such statements symbolically.

Gazing to Stimulate the Soma Chakra

1 *Sit in a comfortable meditation position with your back straight and head erect. Gaze at the tip of your nose with your eyelids half closed (see right). This is called Nasal Gazing (*Nasagra Drishti*). At first, practise for just 10 seconds, then close and relax your eyes. Over time, gradually build up to gazing for 1 minute during a session, but only if your eyes do not feel strained.*

2 *Once you can perform Nasal Gazing without tension, try Frontal Gazing (*Bhrumadhya Drishti*) by looking up toward the centre of your forehead, with your eyelids closed as much as possible. Hold for 10 seconds, then rest your eyes. You may build up to 1 minute of gazing, but prolonged practice is not recommended. You might prefer to practise this exercise with a teacher.*

chapter 7

SAHASRARA CHAKRA
YOUR MYSTICAL CENTRE

Beyond the mind and the intellect, transcending all worldly activities and the awareness of outward appearance, is a plane of timeless existence. Known in Sanskrit as sahasrara, *this is the realm of the crown chakra, the thousand-petalled lotus at the crown of the head that connects your individual awareness with infinite consciousness. Considered to be the highest of the seven major chakras, the sahasrara chakra is also regarded as a gateway to the energy of the universe itself. It is an energetic passageway that leads you from a mundane vision of life to the divine, the collective unconscious and absolute freedom. It is your ladder to immortality. Meditation on the crown chakra works toward realizing the absolute completeness (Brahman) of the yogis, as well as the vision of the void (shunya) of Buddhism.*

Understanding
YOUR SAHASRARA CHAKRA

The crown chakra is the gateway by which your prana, or life-force, enters your chakra system. When undeveloped, this chakra is no larger or more radiant than the other six major energy centres. But, when fully awakened, it is the "mystical centre" and most magnificent of all the chakras, which can be likened to the blaze of a thousand suns shining simultaneously in the sky.

With concerted effort, the unlimited potential energy that lies dormant at your root chakra can be brought to full manifestation at the crown chakra. Indian mythology gives us the image of the serpent force, kundalini, that, once awakened, travels up through the various stages of awareness to the crown chakra, transmuting into the thousand-headed serpent Sesha. At this point, your illusion of being separate from the rest of the universe dissolves.

The crown chakra is your energetic link to expressions of reality that lie beyond the dimensions of everyday existence. As it opens, you become more aware of your multi-dimensional nature. The more balanced your sahasrara energy, the stronger your connection to divine consciousness, in whatever form you see it, whether as a mother or father God, or as Ultimate Reality. As the crown chakra opens, its energy seems to encompass the head. This radiant glow is shown as a halo in images of deities, saints and angels, and may even be the inspiration for the monarch's crown, which symbolizes a fully open and active crown chakra and shows that the sovereign rules with God's grace.

If you are one of the rare people who can access the energy of your crown chakra at will, a feeling of joy will become an integral part of your everyday life. You will receive guidance from higher sources and be drawn toward mystical teachings. Spirituality will become a spontaneous inner experience rather than being mediated by formalized dogma. You might be a visionary, or even considered a miracle worker, able to transcend the laws of nature and access the workings of the unconscious and subconscious mind.

A misaligned crown chakra, however, can cause excessive self-centredness and bring about a narrow vision that makes it difficult to connect with people and the world around you. People with an imbalance in this chakra can be low in energy, or their energy might circulate only in the lower chakras, directed toward materialistic pursuits. Energetic blockages in the crown chakra leave you unreceptive to both the downward flow of energy from higher sources and to the upward flow of energy from the lower chakras. If the crown chakra is even partially blocked, wonder at the richness of the universe will be absent, and creativity will lack inspiration. And people whose sahasrara energy is completely blocked may be unable to see beyond the mundane, be totally materialistic or even be drawn to extremist groups.

Meditating with the crown chakra brings intuitive knowledge, deep understanding, strong spirituality and an enhanced sense of awe. It allows you to connect with other planes of existence and to see the divine interconnectedness of all forms of life.

Working with Sahasrara Energy

As you follow the meditations in this chapter, ask yourself the following questions. They can help you to see how you block your sahasrara energy and to understand how you might rebalance it.

- *Do I crave possessions and sensual pleasures? How can I let go of these cravings?*
- *Do I allow myself to be open to my intuition? How can I do this more?*
- *What would help me to see the world as a manifestation of the divine?*
- *Who am I if I am not limited by this body and this mind?*

Meditating on the Elements:
DISSOLVING THE ELEMENTS

Your physical body is composed of the five elements that make up the universe: earth, water, fire, air and ether (or space). The illusion of this "reality" limits your spirit, and so, in the meditation opposite, known as *Laya Chintana* (Absorbing the Microcosm into the Macrocosm), you envisage each of these physical elements dissolving into and being absorbed by its more subtle neighbour, water evaporating in fire, for example. This enables you to transcend worldly experience and to understand your connection with universal consciousness.

You begin the exercise by thinking about the most solid element, earth, at the root chakra, and visualize it dissolving into water. The water element of the sacral chakra then evaporates in fire; the fire of the solar-plexus chakra merges into the air; the air of the heart chakra disperses into the ether; the ether of the throat chakra is absorbed into the mind at the brow chakra; and finally the mind melds into the absolute consciousness of the crown chakra.

This is the reverse of the process by which the earth was formed. Before our planet became solid, it was liquid (like the molten lava of a volcano). Before it was liquid it was "fire", like the sun. Before this "fire", there was mass of swirling gases (air). Before these gases came into being, they existed as primordial space, which came from the supreme mind – and this was pure consciousness.

Before you begin the meditation opposite, try to memorize its affirmations. If you find this difficult, ask someone else to read them *for* you while you first meditate, or record yourself reading the instructions and then play them back while you meditate.

Laya Chintana Meditation

1 *Sit in a comfortable meditation position, preferably with legs crossed and back straight. Close your eyes and let your breathing settle.*

2 *Mentally repeat to yourself the following sentences one by one:*

"I am not the solid matter of the root chakra. I see earth dissolving in the water of my sacral chakra."

"I am not liquid matter. Water evaporates in fire as I feel my energy ascending to my solar-plexus chakra."

"I am not the element fire. Fire merges into air as my energy rises to my heart chakra."

"I am not gaseous matter. Air disperses in space as my energy rises to my throat chakra."

"I am not the element ether. Ether is a product of the mind. I see space being absorbed back into my mind at my brow chakra."

"Instead of identifying with the limited consciousness of my individual mind, I strive to identify with the cosmos itself. My mind is derived from the universal consciousness. I see it being absorbed back into the universal consciousness at my crown chakra."

3 *Practise for 20 minutes daily, working up to 45 minutes in total. With repeated practice, observe how you begin to experience the interconnectedness of all parts and forms of life.*

"Like bubbles in the water, the worlds rise, exist and dissolve in the Supreme Self, which is the material cause and the prop of everything."
ATMA-BODHA OF SANKARACHARYA, VERSE 8

Mantra Meditation:
THE JEWEL IN THE LOTUS

Each chakra has an associated sound – either a "seed" word or a group of words – that embodies its energy. The mystical energy of the crown chakra is best represented by the mantra *OM MANI PADME HUM*. This is the most widely used of the Buddhist mantras. You do not need any special initiation by a teacher or meditation master in order to use it, nor do you need to be a Buddhist.

Reciting the mantra, aloud or silently, invokes a powerful energy that brings a compassionate and loving relationship with the universe. Looking at its written Tibetan form (see below) has a similar effect. In Tibet, the mantra is carved on stones, engraved on prayer wheels and written on flags so that even the wind carries its energy to the world.

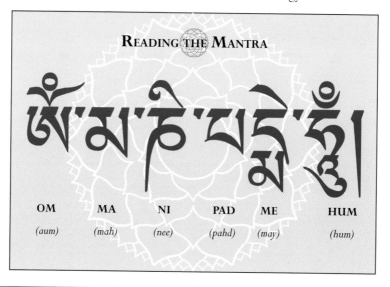

READING THE MANTRA

OM	MA	NI	PAD	ME	HUM
(aum)	(mah)	(nee)	(pahd)	(may)	(hum)

"Above all others is the brilliant thousand-petalled lotus. It is outside this microcosm
of the body and is the giver of salvation."
SIVA SAMHITA, 5.151

Jewel in the Lotus Meditation

---

1 Sit on the floor in front of a low table covered with a clean cloth and place the mantra illustration opposite on it, so that you can see it comfortably. Remove any glasses or contact lenses before beginning this meditation.(If you can't see the mantra illustration well enough, write out the mantra in larger letters.)

2 Sit in a comfortable meditation position, preferably with your legs crossed and back straight. Let your breath settle into a natural rhythm.

3 Start looking at the mantra and read it word by word. As you come to the word PADME, be aware that the translation is "lotus flower". Visualize a brilliant white lotus at your crown centre. The flower is said to have a thousand petals, symbolizing its infinite nature.

4 Read the phrase again, and this time focus on the word MANI, which means "jewel". Visualize your "higher self" as the jewel in the lotus.

5 Repeat the entire mantra out loud several times. Then close your eyes and repeat it silently several times.

6 As you repeat it, visualize yourself sitting on a shimmering lotus with a radiant light emanating from another lotus flower at the crown of your head. Take your awareness to this flower.

7 Continue to repeat the mantra mentally for 20 minutes or longer as you visualize radiance shining out of every cell in your body. Feel as if the mantra is liberating your entire being. Then take a few deep breaths and gently open your eyes.

Progressing further

With continued practice of this meditation, you will begin to experience a sense of expansion and an increased feeling of loving-kindness toward yourself, as well as all other beings. Repeating OM MANI PADME HUM sets you free so that you can help others to be free, too.

Yoga Nidra:
THE COSMIC SLEEP

The practice of *yoga nidra* (cosmic sleep) induces a state of consciousness between waking and sleep that prepares your body to experience deeper levels of awareness and makes your mind sensitive to auto-suggestion. Choose a room free from distractions, and dim the lights, in order to meditate for 20–40 minutes. Ask someone to read out the instructions slowly, or record yourself reading and play it back as you meditate.

Yoga Nidra Meditation

1 *Lie on your back and close your eyes lightly. Rest your arms on the ground with your palms facing upward and let your feet relax to each side. Make this vow to yourself, "I will not sleep, I will remain awake".*

2 *Think about what direction you would like your future to take. For example, would you like to boost your self-confidence? Formulate a resolve regarding these goals, keeping it short and positive. For example your resolve could be:*

"I will be successful in everything I take on."

"I will achieve perfect health."

"I will awaken my spiritual potential."

3 *Take a few deep breaths. As you inhale, feel calm spreading through your body. As you exhale, feel tension flowing away. Be especially aware of your breath as it moves between your navel and your throat. Repeat your resolve mentally three times, with meaning.*

"The Self is the ear of the ear, the mind of the mind, the speech of speech, the life of life and the eye of the eye. Having detached from the sense-organs and renounced the world, the wise attain immortality."
KENA UPANISHAD, 2.2

4 *Direct your focus to each part of your body in turn. Remain alert, but do not try to concentrate. Begin with the right side of your body: the right thumb, index finger, middle finger, ring finger, little finger, palm, back of your hand, wrist, arm, elbow, shoulder, armpit, waist, hip, thigh, kneecap, calf muscle, ankle, heel, sole of your foot, top of your foot and toes. Then repeat this alert focus on your left side.*

5 *Bring your awareness to your back: your shoulder blades, buttocks, spine and then your entire back all at once.*

6 *Be aware of your head: forehead, temples, eyebrows, eyelids, eyes, ears, cheeks, nose, tip of the nose, lips, chin, throat.*

7 *Next, focus on your chest, navel and abdomen, then your entire front. To ward off sleep, repeat, "I am awake, I am practising Yoga Nidra".*

8 *Be aware of the breath coming into your nostrils and moving down your throat to your bronchial tubes and lungs. Then watch your breath as it leaves your body. This completes your physical relaxation.*

9 *Next, relax your emotions. Bring to mind some intense feelings from the past. Try to re-live them and let them go.*

10 *Sense a feeling of lightness, as if your body is made of cotton and is floating. Then feel a heaviness, as if your body is made of lead.*

11 *Witness your awareness within. Repeat the resolve you chose in step 2 a you focus on your crown chakra. Open your eyes, stretch and get up.*

Light Visualization:
AWAKENING THE LIGHT

The sahasrara chakra synchronizes all colours, which is why it manifests as white light. It also fuses all the senses, and with this comes a spiritual connection to the infinite. The aim of the Divine Light Meditation opposite is to use all your powers of imagination to see with your mind's eye a brilliant white light pouring down on you.

During the meditation, you visualize with full concentration the "thousand petals" of the crown chakra opening, just as a flower slowly awakens to morning sunlight. As divine light pours out from between the petals, let it flow freely down through your body. You may practise this exercise alone or with a group of people.

LIGHTING THE WAY FOR OTHERS

If someone you know is in need of help, emotional support or healing, visualize that person rather than yourself being bathed in light during the meditation opposite. See the light entering through the top of his or her head and spiralling downward and say the affirmations using the person's name instead of your own:

"... is surrounded and protected by divine light."

"This light sustains and nourishes his/her entire being."

"... is forever walking in the light."

"... grows stronger by tuning into the divine light."

After blessing your loved one, friend or colleague in this way, give thanks that you are able to share the light. Take a few deep breaths and, when you are ready, open your eyes and slowly stand up.

"Perfect focus on the spiritual light at the top of the head brings visions of realized beings."
PATANJALI, *YOGA SUTRAS*, 3.32

Divine Light Meditation

1 *Sit in a comfortable meditation position, preferably with your legs crossed and your back straight. If working in a group, sit in a circle.*

2 *Rest your hands in your lap, palms upward, with your left hand on top. This is the mudra (hand position) for receiving energy. Close your eyes and let your breathing become slow and even.*

3 *Visualize a myriad-petalled lotus at the crown of your head. Imagine its petals gently opening to reveal an intense light. Let this light flow down into you through your crown chakra. Repeat one of the affirmations below, or create one that has more meaning for you. If you are alone, say the words silently; in a group, you may wish to chant them out loud, in unison:*

"I am surrounded and protected by divine light."

"This light nourishes my entire being."

"I am forever walking in the light."

"I grow stronger by tuning into the divine light."

4 *Feel the light spiralling down your body. Enjoy the warm glow as it saturates your entire being. Let every cell be permeated by light and inspiration, and every part of your consciousness become illuminated.*

5 *Focus your senses on the intensity of the light so that you not only see it, but hear, smell, taste and touch it. Think of the light as a manifestation of your higher self, representing the peace that lies beyond understanding.*

6 *Feel like a pure channel for the light: allow yourself to be at one with it. In this state of oneness, intuitive thoughts and inspirations may enter your consciousness. Be thankful for this guidance.*

7 *After 15–20 minutes, take a few deep breaths, then open your eyes.*

Tools for Working with
SAHASRARA ENERGY

Drawn from complementary therapies, the following tools will support your meditations on the crown chakra. Lotus essence and lavender are particularly good at balancing and enhancing sahasrara energy. If you are pregnant or have a medical condition, consult a medical practitioner before using essential oils or changing your diet.

Flower essences

Place 4 drops under your tongue (or take in water) before meditating.

• CHICORY instils a sense of the oneness and interconnectedness of life.

• MAGNOLIA promotes an inner perspective that encourages you to bring your life into alignment with your highest vision.

• LOTUS opens your crown chakra to universal truths; use 7 drops.

• QUEEN ANNE'S LACE aids your transition to higher consciousness.

Essential oils

Use in a pre-meditation oil bath: blend 3–5 drops of essential oil into 1 tsp carrot seed oil and pour into running water as you fill the bath.

• BRAHMI AYURVEDIC OIL calms and rejuvenates the mind; enhances energy flow at the crown chakra.

• FRANKINCENSE links the sahasrara and muladhara chakras, helping you to resonate on both physical and spiritual levels.

• LAVENDER calms, enabling you to reach deeper states of meditation; helps you to integrate spirituality into your daily life.

• HINA AYURVEDIC OIL warms and rejuvenates to strengthen both body and mind; induces mental clarity; helps to uncover psychic qualities.

"Above all others is the brilliant thousand-petalled lotus. It is ... the giver of salvation."
SIVA SAMHITA, 5.151

• **Spikenard** helps you to connect to the eternal part of yourself that lies beyond the material world (it is the Indian oil of divine anointment).

•**Violet leaf absolute** facilitates your energetic transformation to the higher realms of consciousness.

• **Neroli** encourages your highest aspirations; helps to clear sahasrara energy; reconnects you with your intuition.

Crystals, gems and stones

Wear as jewelry, place near the chakra or just hold before meditation.

• **Amethyst** awakens spirituality and wisdom; for extra potency anoint with 1–2 drops of lavender oil; place the stone near the chakra.

• **Pink calcite** acts as a spiritual amplifier; signifies hope.

• **Citrine** cheers like a golden ray of hope; anoint with 1–2 drops of sandalwood oil to tune into your higher self and attract abundance.

Incense

• **Sandalwood** lifts you to a higher state of consciousness.

• **Cedar** brings clarity of mind and lifts the spirits; infuse with 1 drop of sage oil (*use* Salvia officinalis) to link the crown and root chakras.

• **Frankincense resin** enhances your ability to connect with divinity; has protective properties. Place on charcoal to burn.

• **Myrrh resin** deepens prayer and meditation; helps you toward more profound spiritual connections. Place on charcoal to burn.

• **Copal resin** offers protection and promotes a deeper spirituality. Place on charcoal to burn.

Vegetarian food

A pure, light vegetarian diet is best when working with this chakra.

YOGA ASANA FOR SAHASRARA ENERGY

Often regarded as the quintessence of hatha yoga, *Sirshasana* (Headstand) stimulates the sahasrara energy centre at the crown of your head to enhance clarity of vision and intuition. When you feel ready, progress on from the Half Headstand on pages 136–37 to the full posture shown here. Be sure never to take any weight on your head and shoulders.

Sirshasana: Headstand

Stage 1

Sit on your heels and grasp each elbow with your opposite hand in front of you. Place your arms on the ground. Release your elbows and interlink your fingers to create a tripod shape.

Stage 2

Place your head on the ground with the back of your skull pressing against your clasped hands. Slowly straighten your knees, then walk your feet forward until your hips are directly aligned over your head.

Stage 3

Bend your knees without letting your hips drop. Lift your feet up to your buttocks, keeping your knees bent. Do not jump or use fast movements; come into the pose slowly.

Stage 4

Keeping your knees bent, slowly lift them toward the ceiling.

Stage 5

Gradually straighten your knees, lifting your feet until your body is in a straight line. Hold the position for 30 seconds at the start, gradually building up to 3 minutes. As you hold the pose, make sure that your weight is evenly balanced across both elbows, breathe deeply and take your awareness to your crown chakra. Come down slowly and rest your head on the floor for 3 minutes. Notice how calm you now feel.

GLOSSARY

- *Ajna:* sixth chakra; centre of spiritual energy located between the two eyebrows; the "third eye"
- *Akasha:* space; ether
- *Anahata:* (1) fourth chakra, found at the centre of the body; (2) mystical, soundless sound
- *Anandamaya kosha:* bliss sheath; causal body
- *Annamaya kosha:* food sheath; physical body
- *Asana:* (1) posture; (2) position or pose for meditation and/or body control in hatha yoga
- *Bandha:* (1) lock; (2) muscular lock applied by yogis during certain breathing exercises
- *Bija:* (1) seed or source; (2) bija mantras *LAM, VAM, RAM, YAM, HAM*
- *Brahma granthi:* first psychic knot in the sushumna; located at the muladhara chakra
- *Chakras:* psychic energy centres; located in the sushumna in the astral body
- *Ida:* left nadi, carrying cool, lunar, feminine energy
- *Jnana:* wisdom; knowledge
- *Karma:* action; the law of action and reaction, or cause and effect
- *Karma yoga:* path of selfless service
- *Kosha:* sheath; layer
- *Kundalini:* potential psychic energy; the primordial cosmic energy; from the Sanskrit word *kundala*, meaning "coiled"
- *Manipura:* third chakra, located at the navel centre
- *Manomaya kosha:* mental and emotional sheath in astral body
- *Mantra:* sacred syllable, word or set of words
- *Mouna:* silence as a spiritual practice
- *Mudra:* (1) seal; (2) hatha yoga exercise practised to seal the union of prana (upward-moving vital air) and apana (downward-moving vital air); (3) symbolic hand gesture
- *Mulabandha:* anal lock
- *Muladhara:* first and lowest centre of psychic energy, located at the base of the spine
- *Nadi:* astral nerve, psychic current; equivalent to the meridians of acupuncture
- *Pingala:* right nadi, carrying warm, solar, masculine energy
- *Prana:* life-force; vital energy; equivalent to Chinese *chi* and Japanese *ki*; energy in astral body
- *Pranamaya kosha:* vital sheath in astral body
- *Pranayama:* breathing exercises; control of prana
- *Rudra granthi:* third and final psychic knot in the sushumna; located at the ajna chakra
- *Sahasrara:* thousand-petalled lotus; the highest psychic centre, located at the crown of the head
- *Seed mantra:* one-syllable seed core mantra; *see also bija*
- *Shakti:* (1) power, energy, the goddess; active principle in creation and immanent in it; (2) downward-moving energy within the astral body
- *Siva:* (1) passive, masculine principle; (2) upward-moving energy within the astral body
- *Sushumna:* central nadi, astral tube
- *Swadhisthana:* second chakra, located at the sacral/genital region of the body
- *Uddyana bandha:* abdominal lock
- *Ujjayi breath:* breathing method that works with the throat chakra
- *Vijnanamaya kosha:* intellectual sheath in astral body
- *Vishnu granthi:* second psychic knot in the sushumna; located at the anahata chakra
- *Vishuddha:* fifth chakra, located at the throat
- *Yantra:* mystical diagram or geometric symbol

FURTHER READING

Arewa, Caroline Shola, *Way of the Chakras*, Harper Collins, London, 2001

Avalon, Arthur, *Serpent Power: Secrets of Tantric and Shaktic Yoga*, Dover Publications, New York, 1976

Davis, Patricia, *Subtle Aromatherapy*, C.W. Daniel Co. Ltd., Saffron Walden (UK), 1991

Frawley, Dr David & Lad, Dr Vasant, *The Yoga of Herbs: an Ayurvedic Guide to Herbal Medicine*, Motilal Banarsidass, New Delhi, 2004

Ghosh, Shyam, *The Original Yoga*, South Asia Books, New Delhi, 1980

Gopi, Krishna, *Ancient Secrets of Kundalini*, UBS Publishers/Distributors, New Delhi, 1995

Goswai, Shyam Sundar, *Laya Yoga: the Definitive Guide to the Chakras and Evoking Kundalini*, Inner Traditions/Bear and Company, Rochester VT (USA), 1999

Johari, Harish, *Chakras: Energy Centers of Transformation*, Destiny Books, New York, 2000

Judith, Anodea, *Eastern Body, Western Mind: Psychology and the Chakra System as a Path to the Self*, Celestial Arts, Berkeley CA (USA), 2004

Judith, Anodea, *Wheels of Life: User's Guide to the Chakra System*, Llewellyn Press, Saint Paul MN (USA), 1987

Leadbetter, C.W., *Chakras: A Monograph*, Kessinger Publishing Co., Kila MT (USA), 2003

Miller, Light and Bryan, *Ayurveda and Aromatherapy: the Earth Essential Guide to Ancient Wisdom and Modern Healing*, Motilal Banarsidass, New Delhi, 1998

Mojay, Gabriel, *Aromatherapy for Healing the Spirit*, Gaia Books, London, 2005

Motoyama, Hiroshi, *Theories of the Chakras: Bridge to Higher Consciousness*, Theosophical Publishing House, Wheaton IL (USA), 1981

Myss, Caroline Ph.D, *Anatomy of the Spirit: the Seven Stages of Power and Healing*, Bantam Books, New York, 1997

Northrup, Dr Christiane, *Women's Bodies, Women's Wisdom*, Piatkus Books, London, 1998

Ozanec, Naomi, *Chakras*, Hodder and Stoughton, London, 1988

Salzberg, Sharon, *Loving Kindness: The Revolutionary Art of Happiness*, Shambhala Publications, Boston, 2003

Sivananda, Swami, *Kundalini Yoga*, The Divine Life Society, Rishikesh (India) 1980

Vishnu-devananda, Swami, *Hatha Yoga Pradipika*, OM Lotus Publishing, New York, 1987

FURTHER RESOURCES

• **Chloe Goodchild** relates the chakras to musical notes and body movements: www.thenakedvoice.com

• **Anodea Judith** examines how the chakra system relates to modern Western psychology, somatic therapy and yoga practice: www.sacredcenters.com

• **Caroline Myss** shows how chakra work spans several mystical traditions: www.carolinemyss.com

• **www.namarupa.org** is an online journal of India's sacred philosophical thought

INDEX

ACKNOWLEDGMENTS

PICTURE CREDITS
12 The Art Archive/British Library; **23** Science Photo Library/Garion Hutchings;
27 From "Subtle Body: Essence and Shadow" by David V. Tansley, Thames & Hudson Ltd.
London; **28** The Wellcome Trust, London.

CONTACT THE AUTHOR
Swami Saradananda can be contacted via her website at:
www.FlyingMountainYoga.org

AUTHOR'S ACKNOWLEDGMENTS
I would like to thank my friend Shakti (Dr Shelly Warwick) for always being available to
bounce ideas off.

PUBLISHER'S ACKNOWLEDGMENTS
The publisher would like to thank:
Model: Vicky Cox
Make-up artist: Tinks Reading